Broken Lenses Volume 3

ENDORSEMENTS

As a woman of faith and a sexual assault survivor, I know first-hand how betrayal and trauma can leave us questioning whether God is real, let alone, whether He can heal our pain. *Broken Lenses Volume 3: Experiencing God's Freedom in a World of Sin*, the powerful conclusion to the series, is a practical guide and encouraging resource for anyone who has faced doubt that they matter in the eyes of God.

Emily Bernath examines how we can align our personal values with God's ever-forgiving view of each of us, empowering us to face the voices in the world that would tear us down, to overcome the influences that would leave us believing that we are powerless against the darkness we face, allowing us to finally invest ourselves in an authentic relationship with God.

Angie Fenimore, International Bestselling Author

For anyone who desires a deeper revelation of God's freedom through the word, *Broken Lenses Volume 3* is for you! Thank you, Emily for sharing the hope we have in Christ through your own courageous journey of healing and through simple yet profound passages. Anyone who reads *Broken Lenses* will be encouraged!

Jenna Quinn, MS, Namesake of Jenna's Law & Founder of Reveal to Heal

In *Broken Lenses Volume 3*, Emily continues to take us on a journey of healing. I agree with what she writes in Chapter 7, "If God is light and in him there is no darkness, that means that any area of darkness in our lives that we invite God into cannot stay dark." We are not meant to live our lives without light. Darkness can only remain in the absence of light. Light exists to dispel darkness. Light as an element, impacts or brings change to any environment – after all, who places a light under a basket, when light is to shine. Let God, who is "Light" bring healing and restoration to your life.

Rev Dr Laurie Vervaecke, Staff Pastor, The Well-Salt Lake City, President, Global Leadership Network, Inc., & President, Childhelp Wasatch Front Utah Chapter

Broken Lenses Volume 3: Experiencing God's Freedom in a World of Sin is relatable, equipping, challenging and full of Jesus. Emily Bernath's raw and real look into her own journey of learning the character of God is incredibly refreshing. Her choice to be vulnerable, to ditch the status quo of a carefully crafted persona, and allow us, the readers, a glimpse into her heart and how the love of Jesus has transformed her is something we need more of! I pray this study challenges you to seek the character of God for yourself and that in the seeking, you too experience a life of freedom, conviction, and transformation.

Lauren Snyder, AuD, Team Jesus, Advocate for Overcomers

BROKEN LENSES

—VOLUME 3—

Experiencing God's Freedom in a World of Sin

EMILY BERNATH

NASHVILLE

NEW YORK • LONDON • MELBOURNE • VANCOUVER

Broken Lenses Volume 3

Experiencing God's Freedom in a World of Sin

© 2024 Emily Bernath

Published in New York, New York, by Morgan James Publishing. Morgan James is a trademark of Morgan James, LLC. www.MorganJamesPublishing.com

Proudly distributed by Publishers Group West®

Unless otherwise noted, scripture is taken from the Good News Bible in Today's English Version—Second Edition, Copyright © 1992 by American Bible Society. Used by permission. All rights reserved.

Scripture quotations marked (NIV) are taken from The Holy Bible, New International Version® (NIV®), Copyright © 1973, 1978, 1984, 2011 by Biblica, Inc.™ Used by permission. All rights reserved worldwide.

Scripture quotations marked (ESV) are from The Holy Bible, English Standard Version, Copyright © 2001 by Crossway Bibles, a publishing ministry of Good News Publishers. Used by permission. All rights reserved.

Morgan James BOGO™

A **FREE** ebook edition is available for you or a friend with the purchase of this print book.

_____

CLEARLY SIGN YOUR NAME ABOVE

Instructions to claim your free ebook edition:
1. Visit MorganJamesBOGO.com
2. Sign your name CLEARLY in the space above
3. Complete the form and submit a photo of this entire page
4. You or your friend can download the ebook to your preferred device

ISBN 9781636981130 paperback
ISBN 9781636981147 ebook
Library of Congress Control Number:
2018912159

Cover Design by:
Rachel Lopez
www.r2cdesign.com

Interior Design by:
Christopher Kirk
www.GFSstudio.com

Morgan James PUBLISHING **Builds** with... **Habitat for Humanity®** Peninsula and Greater Williamsburg

Morgan James is a proud partner of Habitat for Humanity Peninsula and Greater Williamsburg. Partners in building since 2006.

Get involved today! Visit: www.morgan-james-publishing.com/giving-back

TABLE OF CONTENTS

Acknowledgments

I started writing the *Broken Lenses* series six and a half years ago, and if I'm honest with you all, a lot of days it still doesn't feel real that God has led me to be an author. I spent twenty years of my life running as far away from books as I could, and if I had things my way, I would probably still be running. As you can see, things in my life didn't go my way, and God has brought much good in my life from the very thing I tried to run away from. I knew very early on in my writing journey that what God was asking me to write would be a three-book series. Seeing that initial commitment that I made to God come to its end is just another testament to the fact that God will never call us to something without giving us everything we need to accomplish it. One of my favorite names for God is Jehovah Jireh, the Lord will provide, and I am forever grateful for all that God has provided to make this journey happen.

To Alyssa, Carly, Danielle, Kaitlyn, Megan, Rachel, and Simile, thank you ladies for taking time out of your schedules each week to invest in both me and my writing. I started writing this book at the beginning of the pandemic in March of 2020, and even when the things of this world were rapidly shifting and uncertain, you adapted as needed to continue to help further my progress of finishing this book. I pray that you all continue to lean on God's sovereign, holy, and miraculous nature to see him work great miracles in your lives and to shine his light brightly through you.

To David, Jim, and the Morgan James Publishing team, thank you for believing in me all these years. Thank you for providing a platform for bringing the calling that God placed on me to life and your support along the way. God knew I was pretty clueless when it came to this whole book publishing thing, so I'm extremely grateful for your expertise and servant heart.

To my parents, I love you and know this journey hasn't been easy for you either, watching your child walk down an unknown path that was never entertained in conversations while growing up. Thank you for your support in that unknown, and I pray you see God's blessing in your own lives as a result of that support.

To my writing coach, Angie, and my editor, Kathryn, thank you for your guidance and support over all these years to help make this book possible. Thank you for believing in my voice before I believed in my own, and instilling the confidence I needed to find that belief.

To the Christian community, both new and old, that God has placed in my life throughout this writing journey, thank you for all of the support and excitement for what God is doing in my life along the way. God doesn't call us to things that we are capable of doing on our own strength, and the journey can get exhausting at times. Seeing the excitement and support given in the community around me provides much needed motivation in those hard moments along the way.

INTRODUCTION

Does God exist? If so, is God someone we should get to know?

I believe that the answer to both of those questions is yes. But I don't want any of you to simply take my word for it. I want you all to experience the goodness of getting to know God for *yourselves*.

If you're reading this book and thinking to yourself, *Yeah, right, God isn't good,* that's okay. I've been there before. I know how it feels to have those thoughts about God, but where do those thoughts come from? Our world has no shortage of opinions on who it thinks God actually is and who God should be, but are any of those opinions true? For all of you who have trouble believing in God's goodness today, I don't expect to be able to magically change your mind. What I *do* expect is for you to at least be willing to read and receive the words in this book with an open mind. Think about it this way: None of us enjoy it when people form perceptions about us without being willing to really get to know who we are. We should offer God that same courtesy.

During my first twenty years of life, if you had asked me if God was someone worth getting to know, my answer would have been somewhere between "not really" or "absolutely not," depending on the day. As those first twenty years of life ended, my animosity toward God reached its peak on the night I was raped.

Within a matter of seconds, my entire life went from *purposeful* to *purposeless*. I found myself hundreds of miles from my community. I had no car, and I was stuck with the man who had just raped me for the rest of the week. How would I ever find purpose again?

In that situation, my mind became overtaken by self-deprecating thoughts. I felt nothing but disgust for my body, and I wanted nothing more than to escape both my mind and my body. I knew that wasn't possible unless I ended my life, and I had no desire to end my life physically. Instead, I escaped my mind and body emotionally by drinking away the pain of the thoughts and disgust.

Talking to God wasn't a regular practice of mine at this point in my life, but, man, did I make sure God heard my anger after being raped. I cried out to him, "What the heck! Are you kidding me? Why did you let this happen, God?" On that night, nothing or no one would have ever stood a chance of convincing me that God possessed *any* goodness. How could God be good *and* allow this to happen to me? That is *exactly* what the enemy of this world wanted me to believe, and the enemy of this world also wants *you* to believe that God can't be good! Why? Because the truth is, God is the *only* one who is good.

> *And as he was setting out on his journey, a man ran up and knelt before him and asked him, "Good Teacher, what must I do to inherit eternal life?" And Jesus said to him, "Why do you call me good? No one is good except God alone." Mark 10:17–18 ESV*

After spending that week with my abuser, I got home and wasted no time sharing with my friends what had happened. I didn't want my friends to think it was okay to hang around someone who thought that raping me was acceptable. I was sure that they would believe me about what had happened, but I was shocked to be proven wrong almost immediately. Not only did some of my friends not believe me, but some told me the rape was *my* fault!

The lack of acceptance and belief by those around me originally sent me further down a drinking spiral and further away from God. But this experience ultimately led me back into a relationship with the one all-loving and true God. I quit hanging out with the people who didn't support me; instead, I surrounded myself with new friends who saw me for my true value and loved me accordingly. It just so happened that those new friends also loved and had a relationship with God.

While I had some apprehension originally about getting to know the God that they all knew so well, I wanted to know more about the love they possessed. I wanted to learn how to love myself again, because regardless of whether I liked it, I had to live with my body for the rest of my life here on this earth.

Who wants to live in constant disapproval and disgust of themselves? No one. Thankfully, none of us has to live that way, because God wants to *free* us from negative views of ourselves and the things that lead us to think that way. The things of this world can try all they want to bring us down, but at the end of the day, they are no match for an all-powerful, all-knowing, and all-loving God.

I no longer see myself as ugly, disgusting, or unworthy because of the trauma I have been through. I know that the God who created me unconditionally loves me and thinks I'm beautiful, and he thinks the same about all of you. I'm not going to sit here and tell you that getting here was easy, but I did keep an open mind, and I was willing to get to know God and invite him into my life. When we do both of those things, there is nothing in our lives that God can't shine his light into.

If you find yourselves surprised at the things you learn about God as you read this book or the things you feel like he's asking you to do, *don't be*. God does not operate in the ways of our world, and he often moves in ways we don't expect. I spent twenty-five years of my life pursuing the "American dream." I moved across the country, got a master's degree, and landed a great-paying job straight out of graduate school. Then God asked me to surrender my career dreams and aspirations to him so I could pursue being an author. *I mean, c'mon, God—are you serious?*

If you know me, you know this might have seemed like cruel and unusual punishment—especially since I hated books throughout my entire childhood. In reality, agreeing to become an author is one of the best things I've ever done in my life. It has opened up doors for me to be God's light to the world through these pages, allows me to be a resource of hope for other sexual assault survivors, and gives more purpose to my life than any job in corporate America ever could have. God knows what he's doing, and he wants the best for you. I pray that as you read this book, you may better come to know the one who loves you more than anything and anyone in this world, and that by gaining a more intimate relationship with God, you come to encounter a freedom unlike anything in this world is able to offer!

The Bible tells us that God is all-knowing, all-powerful, and that there's nothing he is incapable of.

> *If our hearts condemn us, we know that God is greater than our hearts, and he knows everything. 1 John 3:20 NIV*
>
> *"Ah, Sovereign LORD, you have made the heavens and the earth by your great power and outstretched arm. Nothing is too hard for you." Jeremiah 32:17 NIV*
>
> *"For there is nothing that God cannot do." Luke 1:37*

The truth of these verses is either the greatest news or the worst news our world has ever heard, and whether it's the greatest or worst depends on one thing . . . the *nature* of the one who holds that great knowledge, power, and capability. What is God's nature and what does that nature have in store for all of us who are not all-knowing and all-powerful?

> *His divine power has given us everything we need for a godly life through our knowledge of him who called us by his own glory and goodness. Through these he has given us his very great and precious promises, so that through them you may participate in the divine nature, having escaped the corruption in the world caused by evil desires. 2 Peter 1:3–4 NIV*

God's nature is *divine*, and he wants us to participate in this divine nature with him. The only problem? None of us are able to do that on our own. Contrary to the great and precious promises manifested by God's divine nature, our human nature manifests *sin*. In his letter to the Romans, Paul describes this internal conflict that we all face.

> *For I know that good itself does not dwell in me, that is, in my sinful nature. For I have the desire to do what is good, but I cannot carry it out. For I do not do the good I want to do, but the evil I do not want to do—this I keep on doing. Romans 7:18–19 NIV*

Paul speaks of these good desires, but at the end of the day, he is unable to carry those desires out on his own. Instead, he is subject to evil desires that result in the corruption spoken of in Second Peter. If left to fend for himself, the corruption that those evil desires result in would be Paul's end destination. He's not alone: that same corruption would be the end destination for all of us without some kind of intervention.

Thankfully, that corruption from our evil desires doesn't have to have the final say. God's nature is divine, and he wants to *share* the benefits of that divine nature with us, providing us an escape from that corruption! God has no obligation whatsoever to provide us with this escape from the corruption caused by our sin, so why does he?

> *This is love: not that we loved God, but that he loved us and sent his*
> *Son as an atoning sacrifice for our sins. 1 John 4:10 NIV*

God may be all-knowing, all-powerful, and capable of doing whatever he wants to do, but above all else, he is a God of *love*. Because of that love, he wants us to be *free* from the evil and corrupting power of our sin. Out of this great love, God sent Jesus to pay the price we owe for our sins, and the sacrifice Jesus made for our sins is available for all of us to receive.

> *It is for freedom that Christ has set us free. Stand firm, then, and do not*
> *let yourselves be burdened again by a yoke of slavery. Galatians 5:1 NIV*

Freedom is a calling that God desires for every one of us, and the *only* way we can obtain that freedom is through Christ's sacrifice. God's desire for us to be free is so strong that he needed no reason other than the freedom itself to want to set us free from the slavery of sin. What makes freedom such a strong desire of God's? What does possessing this freedom allow us to do?

> *You, my brothers and sisters, were called to be free. But do not use your*
> *freedom to indulge the flesh; rather, serve one another humbly in love.*
> *For the entire law is fulfilled in keeping this one command: "Love your*
> *neighbor as yourself." If you bite and devour each other, watch out or*
> *you will be destroyed by each other. So I say, walk by the Spirit, and*
> *you will not gratify the desires of the flesh. Galatians 5:13–16 NIV*

The freedom we gain by accepting Jesus's sacrifice for our sins and receiving God's Holy Spirit is not an excuse for us to continue living as we please, but rather a calling for us to be an extension of God's love to those around us. How do we love like God loves? We must first get to know who God is.

I pray that this book may equip you to better know and understand the loving, merciful, and miraculous God who reigns over our world. There truly is no one like God, and that is the best news our world has ever heard! God has every right to leave us all to suffer the consequences of our sin for eternity, but he chooses to give us another option because he's a loving Father who wants the best for us.

God sent his only Son to have victory over death and accepting that sacrifice is our only way to escape the corruption of our evil, sinful desires. Accepting the sacrifice Jesus made for us allows us to be an extension of God's light and love for others to this world through the power of his Holy Spirit. God hates seeing us enslaved by our sin, and he wants all of us to be free from it!

I pray you will find that freedom in your lives. With that freedom, I pray you love and serve those around you who need the same hope and freedom that only God can provide.

Chapter One

GOD IS MERCIFUL

Lesson 1: Compassion

Have you ever watched or participated in a sporting event that ended as a result of the *mercy* rule? If you're not familiar with it, the mercy rule applies when one team is so far ahead that the game is ended early to spare the losing team further embarrassment. It's clear who the better team is. How does stopping the game early live up to the rule's name and connect to showing mercy?

> **Mercy:** *noun* compassion shown to an offender; a blessing resulting from divine favor or compassion; compassionate treatment of those in distress[1]

Here we can see a direct correlation between mercy and showing compassion. When it comes to the mercy rule in a sports game, that compassion consists of sparing the losing team from further defeat. While compassion is a key component to showing mercy, the definition doesn't stop there. Mercy isn't about showing compassion to just anybody, mercy specifically involves showing compassion to an *offender*.

This suggests that if God is a merciful God, two things must exist—God must have offenders, and he must also show compassion to those offenders. To understand more about God's merciful nature, we need to know who classifies as God's offenders.

---

1   *Merriam-Webster's Dictionary and Thesaurus,* Updated Edition, s.v. "Mercy."

To be controlled by human nature results in death; to be controlled by the Spirit results in life and peace. And so people become enemies of God when they are controlled by their human nature; for they do not obey God's law, and in fact they cannot obey it. Those who obey their human nature cannot please God. Romans 8:6–8

What do you think it means to be "controlled by our human nature?" How does your own human nature control you?

_____

_____

_____

_____

Anyone who breaks a law offends that law. In that Romans passage, Paul tells us that if we are controlled by our human nature, we *cannot* obey God's law. Since we have all been controlled by our human nature at some point, we have all disobeyed—or been an offender of—God's law. God knows we've all been offenders of his law, but does he show mercy to us and give us compassion in the midst of our offense?

Who is a God like you, who pardons sin and forgives the transgression of the remnant of his inheritance? You do not stay angry forever but delight to show mercy. You will again have compassion on us; you will tread our sins underfoot and hurl all our iniquities into the depths of the sea. Micah 7:18–19 NIV

Why do you think God delights to show us mercy? What does that say about his character?

_____

_____

_____

_____

Not only does God show us compassion—and as a result extend mercy to us—he *delights* in showing us mercy. Why is that?

> **Compassion:** *noun* a strong feeling of sympathy for people who
> are suffering and a desire to help them[2]

Regardless of whether we want to admit it, every one of us experiences suffering and misfortune in this life, and we all need mercy and compassion. I wasn't aware of it at the time, but the night I began pursuing a relationship with God was the same night I went through the deepest level of suffering I've ever experienced.

When it began, that night appeared to be like any other. I found myself with a guy I liked and wanted to work things out with. At that time, things between us in our relationship weren't the best, but there wasn't any one particular reason for that. I was determined I could figure out how to make things good again, and I figured that being on vacation and away from the reality of my everyday life provided a good start to that.

We found some alone time late that night, and in talking about how to make things better, he asked me if I wanted to have sex with him. We had already had this conversation, so he knew where I stood on the matter. I promptly replied with, "I don't think that's a good idea," and I expected the night would continue as usual. Little did I know that he would decide to take matters into his own hands. The next thing I knew, instead of the night continuing as is, I heard the rip of a condom package being opened as he threw himself on top of me.

Instead of enjoying a vacation and life away from reality, I quickly found myself hundreds of miles from home stuck in a room with a man who had just raped me. With no car and no friends who lived nearby, I physically had nowhere else to go. Furious and unable to comprehend what had just happened to me, I looked for someone to talk to other than my abuser. I turned my face to God for the first time in years, pleading, "Why me, God? What did I do to deserve this?"

Before I was raped, I didn't realize it was possible to experience such a depth of suffering. But in that moment, I craved *mercy*. I felt unlovable, my body felt disgusting, and my mind couldn't comprehend how someone could possibly think it was okay to disrespect someone deeply enough to have sex without having con-

---

2   *Oxfordlearnersdictionaries.com*, s.v. "Compassion," accessed December 04, 2022, https://www.oxfordlearnersdictionaries.com/

sent. In my hurt, I needed to know that someone was concerned for me and had compassion toward me, because one thing was for sure—my abuser had neither.

How could you show more compassion or concern for the suffering of the people around you?

_____

_____

_____

_____

Thankfully for us, God willingly steps into that void and shows us mercy and compassion in the midst of our suffering. God gives us compassion and delights to show us mercy because he's a good and loving Father. He is concerned enough about our suffering that he wants to save us from enduring that suffering.

> God will do what is right: he will bring suffering on those who make you suffer, and he will give relief to you who suffer and to us as well. He will do this when the Lord Jesus appears from heaven with his mighty angels, with a flaming fire, to punish those who reject God and who do not obey the Good News about our Lord Jesus. They will suffer the punishment of eternal destruction, separated from the presence of the Lord and from his glorious might, when he comes on that Day to receive glory from all his people and honor from all who believe. You too will be among them, because you have believed the message that we told you. 2 Thessalonians 1:6–10

The suffering that God offers mercy and compassion from isn't just any kind of suffering—it's eternal destruction and separation from both God himself and his goodness. The "Good News about our Lord Jesus" that Paul speaks of is that Jesus came to take care of our offense of God's law. Jesus lived a life free of offending God's law, and he died on the cross so that we don't have to suffer. Jesus's suffering demonstrates compassion and allows us to receive God's mercy for the payment we owe for our sin. His death also gives us a place of eternity in heaven with God rather than being separated from God.

Have you felt the compassion and concern God has for you? If so, how?

_____

_____

_____

_____

How can you give glory and show honor to God in return for the mercy he offers you?

_____

_____

_____

_____

Lesson 2: Blessings

Almost every time I first step outside on a sunny day, I sneeze within a matter of seconds of its rays shining on my face. Should someone else walk by when I sneeze, regardless of whether I've ever met them, they're likely to say either "God bless you" or "Bless you." Saying "bless you" when someone sneezes is such a common gesture in our culture that when the sentiment isn't offered, we might even get caught off guard.

Why is it that we offer a blessing to someone any time they sneeze?

Blessing: _noun_ the invoking of God's favor upon a person[3]

It may seem like a silly example, but the act of blessing someone who sneezes fits the aspect of mercy that that says it's, "a blessing resulting from divine favor or compassion." Regardless of exactly why the tradition started, people believed that something bad happened to a person who sneezed. As a result, we offer blessings to the person who sneezes with the hope that God gives them his mercy by showing divine favor.

---

3   _Dictionary.com,_ s.v. "Blessing," accessed December 04, 2022, https://www.dictionary.com/

How have you been blessed by someone? In what way did they show you compassion?

_____

_____

_____

_____

God loves to bless his children and give favor. In Jesus's famous Sermon on the Mount, he speaks of *mercy* being one of those blessings.

"Blessed are the merciful, for they will be shown mercy." Matthew 5:7 NIV

That verse may sound confusing at first glance—the blessing we receive for showing mercy is also mercy? How does that work? Looking back to the previous lesson, we explored how the merciful are those who show compassion to their offenders. If showing mercy includes showing compassion to our offenders, and mercy is also a blessing received from showing compassion, that means that mercy can be received as an act of us being merciful.

How have you received mercy as a result of being merciful to someone else?

_____

_____

_____

_____

Being merciful is the very essence of God's character—he *never* stops extending mercy to us.

The steadfast love of the LORD never ceases; his mercies never come to an end; they are new every morning; great is your faithfulness. Lamentations 3:22–23 ESV

God can't help but be a merciful God. Showing mercy comes as a natural response to his steadfast love. While none of us possesses a nature that loves and shows mercy, when we possess God's Spirit, we gain the power to be people who can extend his mercy to others. Jesus provides us with an example of how to bless others and show that mercy in the following passage:

> *"If you love only the people who love you, why should you receive a blessing? Even sinners love those who love them! And if you do good only to those who do good to you, why should you receive a blessing? Even sinners do that! And if you lend only to those from whom you hope to get it back, why should you receive a blessing? Even sinners lend to sinners, to get back the same amount! No! Love your enemies and do good to them; lend and expect nothing back. You will then have a great reward, and you will be children of the Most High God. For he is good to the ungrateful and the wicked. Be merciful just as your Father is merciful." Luke 6:32–36*

Why do you think Jesus says, "even sinners do that" after each of the first three comparisons?

_____

_____

_____

_____

At the end of that passage, Jesus calls us again to be merciful people. Jesus speaks of loving others, doing good, and lending to others in the context of receiving a blessing. The blessing he speaks of doesn't come from where we might like it to, though. Loving those who love us and doing good to those who do good to us requires little to no sacrifice on our end. Instead, he calls us to show mercy by doing good to our enemies and lending to others without expecting to get paid back. Sounds easy enough, right?

Of course it's not.

After being raped, I spent the rest of that vacation as far away from my abuser as possible. When the vacation finally ended, I had to ride in the same car for twelve hours with the man who raped me just days earlier. It was the longest car ride of my life, to say the least.

When I got home, I was not quiet in telling my friends about what happened while we were gone. Why? I expected people to show *mercy* to me. Little did I know how much my expectations would be left unmet. Rather than receiving mercy and people wanting to bless me in a time of deep hurt, I got told it was my fault!

I endured a lot of loss in a short amount of time, especially when it came to things like my friendships, self-confidence, and joy. I distanced myself from as many unsupportive people and activities as I could. After about a month and a half of not saying anything to my abuser, I gained the confidence to talk to him as an act of wanting to extend forgiveness. I wasn't attempting to forget what he did or say that what he did to me was okay, because it wasn't. I knew that he would never be able to repay me for all that he took away from me, but I also knew that repaying evil with evil would lead to nowhere good. I did not want to allow what he did to me to have control over my life.

Although we've all gone through our various trials and pains in life, I'm betting that you could name at least one person who has been good to you. Is that the only person you should show goodness to? If God took on that same mindset and did good only to those who were good to him, he'd be good to *nobody*!

We have all at some time betrayed God. Thankfully, we have a God who is merciful and is so good that he sacrificed his own Son's life for ours, even though we're not good to him. That same mercy and sacrifice allows us to receive the greatest blessing there is—becoming children of God and being born again through his Spirit.

Who or what are you hesitating to love or do good for in your life right now and why?

Recall a time when you loved, did good for, or lent something to someone without expecting them to return it to you. What impact did that act of mercy have on that situation?

_____

_____

_____

_____

Lesson 3: Divine

All of us at some point in life come to a place where we need the help of another person to accomplish a task. Often times, those tasks remain unaccomplished because we don't ask for the help we need.

What is it that holds us back? There are a variety of things. Sometimes we don't personally know someone who can provide us with the help we need. Other times, we do know a person who could help us, but we don't want to ask them. And even when we know a person who could help and we do want to ask them, we still don't ask them at times because our world places a stigma on needing help.

Many times, another person can provide us with the help we need. If we're moving into a new home, we seek the favor of people who are willing to donate their time and strength to help us move our heavy items. If we're going out of town, we seek the favor of someone to watch our pets and belongings while we're away. In situations like these, it's relatively easy to find a person who can fulfill the favor we need.

What is a favor you need right now? Is there anything preventing you from asking someone to help you? Why or why not?

_____

_____

_____

_____

Even though we are all capable of doing many things, we're all still human, and we have limitations. If we didn't have limitations, we would never encounter a situation where we needed a favor. Our limitations don't just limit our capabilities, but they also limit the types of favors we're able to do for others. Mercy is one of those favors. What makes us unable to show mercy? Mercy isn't like other favors that we can do on our own strength. Why? The definition of *mercy* states that mercy is a *divine* favor.

Divine: *adjective* of superhuman or surpassing excellence; proceeding from God or a god[4]

Why is it important to make the distinction that mercy requires divine favor? Because it means we need something *superhuman* to provide mercy. God alone contains those superhuman abilities and provides mercy within his nature, and if we want to be merciful as well, we need *his* strength.

How have you seen God's superhuman or surpassing excellence provide favor in your life? What freedom came as a result of that mercy?

_____

_____

_____

_____

There are some favors we will never be able to provide for people without God's surpassing excellence, and that's okay. God doesn't ask us to be God; he asks us to have faith and trust in him.

Then they came to Jericho. As Jesus and his disciples, together with a large crowd, were leaving the city, a blind man, Bartimaeus (which means "son of Timaeus"), was sitting by the roadside begging. When he heard that it was Jesus of Nazareth, he began to shout, "Jesus, Son of David, have mercy on me!" Many rebuked him and told him to be quiet, but he shouted all the more, "Son of David, have mercy on me!"

---

4   *Dictionary.com*, s.v. "Divine," accessed December 04, 2022, https://www.dictionary.com/

Jesus stopped and said, "Call him." So they called to the blind man,
"Cheer up! On your feet! He's calling you." Throwing his cloak aside,
he jumped to his feet and came to Jesus. "What do you want me to do
for you?" Jesus asked him. The blind man said, "Rabbi, I want to see."
"Go," said Jesus, "your faith has healed you." Immediately he received
his sight and followed Jesus along the road. Mark 10:46–52 NIV

In this passage, a blind man, Bartimaeus, seeks divine favor and asks Jesus to have mercy on him. After Bartimaeus makes this cry to Jesus, two very different responses occur. The first response comes from the crowd of people. The crowd demonstrates a perfect example of our selfish human nature. Here in front of them is a man begging for mercy, and how do they respond? They rebuke Bartimaeus and tell him to be quiet. Not very merciful, is it?

As a survivor of sexual assault, I had a deep craving for mercy, but I did not look for mercy from the right people or in the right places. I found myself in a similar place as Bartimaeus, begging to God. However, rather than begging God for mercy, I simply begged to know what I did to deserve such pain. Outside of my initial cry to God the night it happened, my other cries for mercy were to the people in my life at the time. The only problem with that approach? None of them were superhuman, and I also hadn't spent my life investing in God-centered friendships.

Those people were incapable of showing the mercy that God's divine power possesses. Rather than showing mercy, they did just as the people in this passage did—they rebuked me and tried to quiet me by saying it was my fault. On top of that, when I went to talk to my abuser after he raped me, I found out he started dating someone else that he knew through me. This forced me further down a path of isolation and desperation.

Do you ever find yourself responding in a way similar to the crowd's response in your own life? If so, what was the situation?

_____

_____

_____

_____

The other response to Bartimaeus comes from Jesus. Jesus hears the exact same cry for mercy that the crowd heard, yet he responded very differently. He stops right where he's at, calls Bartimaeus over, and *listens* to him. He takes the time to hear Bartimaeus and to ask what he wants. Jesus immediately extends mercy and divine favor to Bartimaeus by healing him as a result of his faith.

As painful as the rejection, lack of mercy, and isolation from my friends were, I did not allow their actions to silence me from sharing what happened that night. A few months later, I started to make new friends, and in doing so I was open about where I was in life and what had happened to me. One of these new friends coincidentally knew the same people who had told me that the rape was my fault. Rather than passing blame or judgment onto me, they reacted the way Jesus did to Bartimaeus. They stopped what they were doing and listened. By taking time out of her day to see me in my hurt and to hear my needs, I could immediately see something different in her. That difference shined a ray of light into the very dark place to which life had led me and left me with a sense of hope.

If Jesus asked you the same question that he asked Bartimaeus, "What do you want me to do for you?" what would you say?

_____

_____

_____

_____

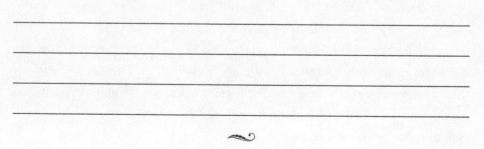

Lesson 4: Distress

None of us has to look very far before we see a person in distress. The cause of that person's distress could come from a variety of sources and could be physical, emotional, or spiritual. Regardless of the cause of the distress, the pains of distress are very real.

Any time we come across someone with distress, we have an opportunity to show *mercy*, which is partly defined as "compassionate treatment of those in distress."[5] How do we know when we have an opportunity to show that kind of mercy?

Distress: *noun* suffering of body or mind; a condition of danger or desperate need[6]

Sin causes suffering in this world, and the distress of that suffering is not going to go away until heaven and earth are restored. This means that there are countless opportunities for us to extend mercy and show compassion to those around us in distress.

What was a time in your life when you felt distress? Did anyone show you compassion in that situation? If so, how did they make you feel?

_____

_____

_____

_____

Where do you see suffering, danger, or desperate need happening in this world? How can you show compassion to those who are being affected by it?

_____

_____

_____

_____

The sexual assault I endured caused me distress—or suffering of body and mind—that I never before knew was possible. I hated being in my own body. My mind consisted of nonstop toxic thoughts telling me, *I am no longer as worthy or beautiful as I used to be.* Aside from medicating my pain with alcohol, I had no other escape from those thoughts of disgust for myself.

---

5   *Merriam-Webster's Dictionary and Thesaurus,* Updated Edition, s.v. "Mercy."
6   *Merriam-Webster's Dictionary and Thesaurus,* Updated Edition, s.v. "Distress."

Thankfully, God did not allow the alcohol or my negative thoughts to have the final say in my life. I learned that having a relationship with God was possible because the new friends I made showed me compassion in my distress. One of them invited me into her life by asking if I wanted to go to church with her. After so much loss in relationships and any sense of self-confidence I once had stripped away from me, I desperately needed connection and to know that I was still loved.

Showing compassion to those in distress requires us to acknowledge the needs of others above our own. Unfortunately, our human nature tends to dwell on our own needs and overlook the needs of others. God is well aware of that tendency of our human nature, so he extends mercy on our behalf. God *loves* to help us in our troubles!

> *Let us give thanks to the God and Father of our Lord Jesus Christ, the merciful Father, the God from whom all help comes! He helps us in all our troubles, so that we are able to help others who have all kinds of troubles, using the same help that we ourselves have received from God. 2 Corinthians 1:3–4*

How could you use God's help right now?

_____

_____

_____

_____

God is not only is a merciful Father, but he also helps us show mercy to others. How does a good and mighty God know how to show compassion to those who are suffering and in distress? He knows because he has felt the same suffering, and he sent his Son to earth to endure the trouble brought on by our sin.

> *Just as we have a share in Christ's many sufferings, so also through Christ we share in God's great help. If we suffer, it is for your help and salvation; if we are helped, then you too are helped and given the strength to endure with patience the same sufferings that we also endure. So our hope in you is never shaken; we know that just as you share in our sufferings, you also share in the help we receive. 2 Corinthians 1:5–7*

Through Jesus's distress and suffering in this world, God both shows us mercy and helps us to show mercy to others. By his strength, we are able to endure the sufferings of this world and know how to have compassion for others who are suffering.

I said yes to my friend's invitation to join her at church for a couple of reasons. The first reason was that all of the hope I once had was shaken by the sexual assault. I did not know how to escape the darkness in my life. When I saw someone else willing to go out of their way to make sure I was seen and to include me in something, I caught a glimpse of hope that had been lost for months. The second reason I accepted my friend's invitation was because the only solutions I had for my suffering were anything but sustainable. Getting drunk to forget about my suffering worked for a few hours, but it also created a far from enjoyable hangover the next morning.

Little did I know that I didn't need to find sufficiency from anything of this world. God's mercy and compassion for those in distress is sufficient for everyone. He is the only one we can place our hope in and have assurance that we will not be shaken.

What do you think it means to share in Christ's sufferings?

_____

_____

_____

_____

How have you shared in Christ's sufferings, and what strength did you need to endure it?

_____

_____

_____

_____

Dear God,

Thank you for being a God of mercy. You willingly extend your compassion to all who have offended you, including me. Your love for me is so great that you not only want to show me mercy, but you delight in it. Help me to be a person who extends that same mercy and compassion to others. You love your enemies and do good to others without expecting anything in return, and you call me to do the same. I confess that I am often too concerned with my own needs to be looking for opportunities to show mercy to others. In reality, I have no need to be concerned, because you already know what I need. No suffering on this earth goes unnoticed by you. You love to help all of us in our troubles. Because of the help you have given me, I am able to help others with those same troubles. Your mercy and compassion will always be enough to help me endure any trial on this earth, and anything telling me otherwise is a lie. You are the only one in whom I can place my hope and know that I won't be shaken.

In Jesus' name,
Amen.

Chapter Two

GOD IS MARVELOUS

Lesson 1: Wonder

If I asked a believer of God, "Do you think God is good?" I have great confidence that believer would say, "Yes." If I asked that same person, "Do you think God is *marvelous*?" I'm not quite as confident the answer would be "yes." Why? The concept of *good* and *bad* is widely understood and learned at an early age. Becoming a believer of God requires us to put our faith in God, and I can't say I've met anyone who has done that and also thinks God is "bad." But believing that God is marvelous requires us to have more than just an understanding of good and bad—we must realize how *big* God is and what he's capable of doing.

> *Now to him who is able to do far more abundantly than all that we ask or think, according to the power at work within us, to him be glory in the church and in Christ Jesus throughout all generations, forever and ever. Amen. Ephesians 3:20–21 ESV*

How is God's power at work within you?

_____

_____

_____

_____

How are you bringing or how can you bring glory to God as a result of that work?

_____

_____

_____

_____

God is capable of doing more than we could ever imagine. When we witness him doing work that he alone can do, we can't help but *marvel* at his greatness.

> *The LORD says, "My servant will succeed in his task; he will be highly honored. Many people were shocked when they saw him; he was so disfigured that he hardly looked human. But now many nations will marvel at him, and kings will be speechless with amazement. They will see and understand something they had never known." Isaiah 52:13–15*

In this passage, God gives a foreshadowing of Jesus. Jesus came to this earth not with the task of being served, but to serve and give his life as a sacrifice for many. He was whipped, nailed to a cross, and died for the sins of all who would ever live on this earth. After that, Jesus did as *only* he can do and rose from the grave—how marvelous is that?

Marvelous: *adjective* causing wonder[7]

The marvelous nature of Jesus didn't begin when he died for our sins. Jesus instilled wonder in people everywhere he went:

> *As soon as all the people saw Jesus, they were overwhelmed with wonder and ran to greet him. Mark 9:15 NIV*

The mere *presence* of Jesus was enough to fill the people with wonder. Why do you think that is?

Wonder: *noun* a cause of astonishment or admiration[8]

---

7 *Merriam-Webster.com*, s.v. "Marvelous," accessed December 04, 2022, https://www.merriam-webster.com/

8 *Merriam-Webster.com*, s.v. "Wonder," accessed December 04, 2022, https://www.merriam-webster.com/

Has encountering Jesus ever overwhelmed you with wonder? If so, how?

_____

_____

_____

_____

Even though being in the presence of Jesus overwhelmed people with wonder, Jesus didn't stop his marvelous ways there. Among that group of people from the passage in Mark stood a father whose son was possessed by an evil spirit. Jesus continued to marvel the people by casting out the spirit.

> Jesus asked the boy's father, "How long has he been like this?" "From child-hood," he answered. "It has often thrown him into fire or water to kill him. But if you can do anything, take pity on us and help us." "'If you can'?" said Jesus. "Everything is possible for one who believes." Immediately the boy's father exclaimed, "I do believe; help me overcome my unbelief!" When Jesus saw that a crowd was running to the scene, he rebuked the impure spirit. "You deaf and mute spirit," he said, "I command you, come out of him and never enter him again." Mark 9:21–25 NIV

At first, the boy's father is apprehensive and unsure of Jesus. He says that _if_ Jesus can do anything, take pity on him, and help heal his son. Jesus responds to the father's apprehension by showing him the marvelous power of God.

By walking back into a church in a season of darkness and deep pain, I found myself in a situation similar to the boy's father. The only reason I turned to God to begin with was because I had nowhere else to go and no one else to turn to. I held no belief in the fact that God could heal me. In my mind, my body had been permanently tainted and its value would never amount to any level of value I saw in it before I was assaulted. While I had no belief that healing was possible, I did not want the pain I suffered to be my reality for the rest of my life. If God could actually do it, I wanted him to have pity on me, but wanting God to have pity on me is where my similarity to the father in this passage stopped.

After Jesus said that everything is possible for those who believe, the father's character shifted. The father went from "kind of" believing to being marveled and wanting to overcome his unbelief. He was astonished by Jesus's proclamation and admired Jesus's willingness to heal his son. In his marvel, the father believed, and Jesus healed his son through the power of prayer.

Unlike the boy's father, the unbelief I carried in my heart was too strong to even allow God to respond to my cry for pity. When I asked God to have pity on me, I didn't believe that would actually happen; instead, I used it as an avenue to get my extreme anger off my chest. In my mind, healing wasn't possible, so I didn't allow much space in my heart to have any belief in God's healing power.

What do you admire about God and why?

_____

_____

_____

_____

Where do you have unbelief right now? How can God help you overcome your unbelief?

_____

_____

_____

_____

Lesson 2: Amazing

The word *amazing* gets used constantly in our world to describe things. We use this word so often that I think we become slightly numb to the depth of its meaning. We find *amazing* among the list of synonyms of *marvelous*[9], but how often when we say something is *amazing* do we also think it's *marvelous*?

---

9   *Merriam-Webster.com*, s.v. "Marvelous," accessed December 04, 2022, https://www. merriam-webster.com/

God is nothing short of amazing, but what does that mean?

Amazing: *adjective* causing amazement, great wonder, or surprise[10]

Amazing is a term that has been used for centuries to describe God, and it finds its way into the title of arguably the most popular hymn in the world—"Amazing Grace." What makes God's grace so amazing? Contrary to the extremely works-focused world in which we live, the Bible tells us that it is not through our works, but by God's grace alone that we are saved.

> *For by grace you have been saved through faith. And this is not your own doing; it is the gift of God, not a result of works, so that no one may boast. Ephesians 2:8–9 ESV*

How could you use God's grace right now?

_____

_____

_____

_____

Has God's grace ever caused amazement or surprise in your life? If so, how?

_____

_____

_____

_____

One of my favorite lines in "Amazing Grace" says, "How precious did that grace appear the hour I first believed." Why? Just as I think our world has lost sight on what "amazing" means, I think we often forget the amazing nature of God's grace.

> *For the grace of God has appeared that offers salvation to all people. Titus 2:11 NIV*

---

10 *Merriam-Webster's Dictionary and Thesaurus,* Updated Edition, s.v. "Amazing."

Without me even knowing it at the time, God offered his grace to me in the form of the new friendships I gained from starting to attend church again. Because I had such little faith in God's healing power, I relied on myself to remedy my pain, and I did that by turning to alcohol. I wasn't willing to give up drinking even after I started attending church. Instead, I did both. I often went to church hungover from the night before. While getting drunk never actually healed my pain, it at least provided a way to forget about the pain for a few hours. Had I been left to figure life out on my own, this path of drinking is likely the path my life would've continued to take, and there's no telling if I ever would have found healing.

God's graciousness offers healing to everyone. It is the *only* reason any of us can gain salvation and be forgiven of our sin. When we realize that for the first time and believe in Jesus as our savior, it is nothing short of an *amazing* experience.

Even though we are good at forgetting about the amazing qualities of God, that doesn't take away from the fact that amazing is part of his character. When we see God at work, it's guaranteed to be amazing.

> *One day Jesus said to his disciples, "Let us go over to the other side of the lake." So they got into a boat and set out. As they sailed, he fell asleep. A squall came down on the lake, so that the boat was being swamped, and they were in great danger. The disciples went and woke him, saying, "Master, Master, we're going to drown!" He got up and rebuked the wind and the raging waters; the storm subsided, and all was calm. "Where is your faith?" he asked his disciples. In fear and amazement they asked one another, "Who is this? He commands even the winds and the water, and they obey him."*
> Luke 8:22–25 NIV

In this passage, the disciples' faith gets tested. They had enough faith in Jesus to get in the boat and go to the other side of the lake, but once the storm came in, they lost their faith. Instead of having the peace of knowing Jesus was with them, they began to worry, and they woke Jesus up. Jesus surprised the disciples by calming the wind and the water, and they couldn't help but stand in amazement.

Similar to the disciples, I had enough faith to "get in the boat" and attend church again, but when the storms of life hit, I lost my faith. When the thoughts of worthlessness and disgust attacked me, I placed my faith in alcohol and turned to the bottle to escape from the pain. God knew that I put more faith in alcohol than I put in him, and he essentially asked me, "Where is your faith, Emily?" by making it so that I could no longer have even one drink without getting ill. Initially, I stayed stubborn in my ways and kept drinking despite the physical and emotional pain it caused. Unless God could show me that he could bring peace and calmness to the destructive thoughts that consumed my mind, I remained unwilling to give up the faith I placed in alcohol.

God alone contains the power to calm the wind and the waves. Just like he had control over the storm then, he has control over all of the storms we face in life now. Following God is a *journey*, and it's a journey that requires faith. Each time we say "yes" to God, we take a step of faith in that journey. Taking steps of faith puts us in a place to be blown away by God's amazing goodness and provision. When we allow God to work in our lives, we get the pleasure of both witnessing and being amazed by works only he can do.

Has God amazed you with his provision in a step of faith you've taken? If so, how?

_____

_____

_____

_____

What does your journey with God look like right now?

_____

_____

_____

_____

Lesson 3: Stunning

All of us have been stunned by something at some point, whether in a good or bad way. When something stuns us, it catches us off guard.

We often view the word *stunning* in reference to physical beauty. Our world holds many opinions on what is and is not stunning when it comes to physical beauty, and it does not relent in making sure we know those opinions. Living up to the world's expectations for being physically stunning is a lofty task that is near impossible to live up to.

Following my sexual assault, I felt like my physical beauty had been stripped from me. God knew how I felt about my physical beauty following my sexual assault, but he did not feel the same way. God created each of us in his image, and his image is one of beauty. I wasn't immediately convinced of the beauty God saw in me, but I *wanted* to see it, and that kept me going to church. Ultimately, the drinking and other things of this world that I looked to for fulfillment left me empty-handed the next day and looking for more. I grew tired of constantly feeling empty and unfulfilled, so I eventually listened to my body's reactions to alcohol and stopped drinking so heavily.

Although it took years to break the chain of being unable to see my beauty, God never stopped pursuing me. We obviously can't physically see God himself here on earth, but that doesn't take away from his stunning nature. For this lesson, we will focus on a different type of stunning:

Stunning: *adjective* causing astonishment or disbelief[11]

When God works, he always causes astonishment. Jesus caused astonishment during his ministry on earth. His ways of ministering were not what people expected when they pictured what the long-awaited and prophesied messiah would be like—but we should always remember that God's ways are *not* our ways.

> *For my thoughts are not your thoughts, neither are your ways my ways,*
> *declares the LORD. For as the heavens are higher than the earth, so are*
> *my ways higher than your ways and my thoughts than your thoughts.*
> *Isaiah 55:8–9 ESV*

---

11 *Merriam-Webster's Dictionary and Thesaurus,* Updated Edition, s.v. "Stunning."

What does God mean when he says his thoughts and ways are not the same as ours?

_____

_____

_____

_____

How are God's thoughts and ways different from your thoughts or ways?

_____

_____

_____

_____

Jesus made sure to shine light on this truth that God declared through Isaiah by showing us that his ways are not our ways. One example of Jesus showing this difference is illustrated in the following passage:

> _And behold, a man came up to him, saying, "Teacher, what good deed must I do to have eternal life?" And he said to him, "Why do you ask me about what is good? There is only one who is good. If you would enter life, keep the commandments." He said to him, "Which ones?" And Jesus said, "You shall not murder, You shall not commit adultery, You shall not steal, You shall not bear false witness, Honor your father and mother, and, You shall love your neighbor as yourself." The young man said to him, "All these I have kept. What do I still lack?" Jesus said to him, "If you would be perfect, go, sell what you possess and give to the poor, and you will have treasure in heaven; and come, follow me." When the young man heard this he went away sorrowful, for he had great possessions. Matthew 19:16–22 ESV_

Here we have a man approaching Jesus, looking for the answer to gaining eternal life. He tries to gain eternal life through his good deeds. He asks Jesus what good deed he needs to do, and Jesus quickly shows the young man how his ways are different. Jesus tells the young man that inherently the young man isn't good, and Jesus speaks of God when he says, "There is only one who is good." Trying to gain eternal life by good deeds alone *isn't possible!*

Jesus then continues by laying out the action-steps the man can take to gain eternal life; he asks the young man to sell his possessions and follow him. If the young man did this, he would then have treasures in heaven. This scenario of giving up possessions is an all-familiar scenario for those who are followers of Christ. God often tests our faith by asking us to give up something in order to follow him. It's not easy, but if God is the most important thing in our lives, then it's worth it to give up everything he asks to follow him. This requires us to have faith and believe that God's ways are higher than ours.

Giving up drinking as a source of fulfillment was far from easy, but it was a lot more do-able once I had a group of Christian friends by my side—friends who loved me as I was, not after I had loosened up from a few beers. I didn't know what I was getting myself into by saying yes to God and no to alcohol and getting more involved in church. What I *did* know is that saying yes to alcohol for three years straight had done nothing but leave me feeling empty. Although the *urge* to drink proved difficult to give up, it was easy to want to leave behind the *results* of the drinking.

What has God asked you to give up in order to follow him?

_____

_____

_____

_____

Following his interaction with the young man, Jesus continues to explain the differences between God's ways and ours.

And Jesus said to his disciples, "Truly, I say to you, only with difficulty will a rich person enter the kingdom of heaven. Again I tell you, it is easier for a camel to go through the eye of a needle than for a rich person to enter the kingdom of God." When the disciples heard this, they were greatly astonished, saying, "Who then can be saved?" But Jesus looked at them and said, "With man this is impossible, but with God all things are possible"... "But many who are first will be last, and the last first." Matthew 19:23–26,30 ESV

Jesus stunned, or *marveled*, the disciples by greatly astonishing them with his description of how difficult it is for rich people to get into heaven. He made it clear that it is *only* by God's doing that we can be saved. No amount of wealth or possessions can buy our way into the kingdom of God; our access into the kingdom of God was bought by the blood of Jesus.

Unlike the way of the world, the way of God demonstrates that the first will be last and the last first. Jesus didn't come to the earth to be served but to serve, and he calls us to have the same kind of mentality. Our faithfulness to God does not go unnoticed. When we give up what God asks of us to follow him, he provides for us and astonishes us with his ways.

What do you think Jesus means when he says, "the first will be last and the last first?"

_____

_____

_____

_____

How can you apply that same kind of mentality in your own life?

_____

_____

_____

_____

Lesson 4: Phenomenal

We live in a culture that often discourages being "unusual." The media paints a picture of what our lives and physical appearance should look like, and then it judges how good we are at achieving those images. The problem with this mentality? It doesn't line up with God's intention of creating us. The world likes to say that being unusual is a "bad" thing, but on what does our world base that judgment?

The next synonym for *marvelous* I want us to explore is *phenomenal*.[12] Part of what it looks like to be phenomenal includes the concept of being unusual.

> **Phenomenal:** *adjective* relating to or being a phenomenon; so unusual as to be remarkable[13]

How do we know when we've seen something phenomenal? The Bible challenges our viewpoint on what is and isn't unusual.

> *My dear friends, do not be surprised at the painful test you are suffering, as though something unusual were happening to you. Rather be glad that you are sharing Christ's sufferings, so that you may be full of joy when his glory is revealed. Happy are you if you are insulted because you are Christ's followers; this means that the glorious Spirit, the Spirit of God, is resting on you. 1 Peter 4:12–14*

We see here what *shouldn't* be considered unusual—going through painful tests and suffering. We will all experience times of pain and suffering on this earth, and none of us is "unusual" because of them.

What *is* unusual is how Peter describes handling the pain and suffering. Peter declares that we are to be *glad* when we share in Christ's suffering—but why? First, I want to be clear that while we should be glad to share Christ's sufferings, I am not saying that suffering isn't a big deal or something we should just "get over." Nor am I saying that we should create as much suffering as possible. As long as we are in this world and separated from God, suffering will exist—but we don't have to allow that suffering to define us.

---

12 *Merriam-Webster's Dictionary and Thesaurus,* Updated Edition, s.v. "Marvelous."
13 *Merriam-Webster's Dictionary and Thesaurus,* Updated Edition, s.v. "Phenomenal."

What is a painful test that God is taking or has taken you through?

_____

_____

_____

_____

How can you consider pain and suffering you've been through as a reason to be glad in sharing Christ's sufferings?

_____

_____

_____

_____

As followers of Christ, we have the glorious Spirit of God with us—the same Spirit that allows us to continue to do phenomenal works like Christ did while on earth. Pain and suffering allow us to experience tests of faith. The enemy tries to convince us to doubt having faith in God—how could God both be good and allow suffering? The truth is, not only is God good all the time, but when we place our faith in him, _remarkable_ things happen.

> _Some men came carrying a paralyzed man on a mat and tried to take him into the house to lay him before Jesus. When they could not find a way to do this because of the crowd, they went up on the roof and lowered him on his mat through the tiles into the middle of the crowd, right in front of Jesus. When Jesus saw their faith, he said, "Friend, your sins are forgiven." The Pharisees and the teachers of the law began thinking to themselves, "Who is this fellow who speaks blasphemy? Who can forgive sins but God alone?" Jesus knew what they were thinking and asked, "Why are you thinking these things in your hearts? Which is easier: to say, 'Your sins are forgiven,' or to say, 'Get up and walk'? But I want you to know that the Son of Man has authority on earth to forgive sins." So he said to the paralyzed_

man, "I tell you, get up, take your mat and go home." Immediately he stood up in front of them, took what he had been lying on and went home praising God. Everyone was amazed and gave praise to God. They were filled with awe and said, "We have seen remarkable things today." Luke 5:18–26 NIV

This passage starts with some men on a mission to get a paralyzed man to Jesus. On their way, they experience roadblocks, but they do not let that stop their effort to get the man to Jesus.

As I went back to church and tried to overcome drinking, I found myself in a place similar to the paralyzed man in the passage. My paralysis, however, was not physical but was emotional. Nothing about getting so drunk that you can barely make out complete thoughts or having a hangover the next day is physically enjoyable. But the physical pain of a hangover did not come close to the emotional pain that I covered up, or paralyzed, by drinking.

I wasn't sure if there was something out there that would do more than just mask my pain. Then I found that the community I built in church was sure, and my friends there played the role of the men carrying the paralyzed man on the mat. I had lost my self-worth and my old community in a short period of time, bringing me to a very painful and isolating time in my life, but my friends at church provided me with a place of welcome and a place to encounter Jesus.

What is a roadblock have you had to overcome in your pursuit of Jesus, and how did you overcome it?

After the men successfully got the paralyzed man in front of Jesus, Jesus acknowledges their faith and forgives the paralyzed man of his sins. The Pharisees immediately doubt Jesus's ability to forgive sins, saying that only God can forgive sins. Jesus addresses their doubt and instructs the paralyzed man to walk. When the crowd sees a formerly paralyzed man walk, they acknowledge the *phenomenal* nature of God and praise God for the remarkable works they witness.

God is just as capable of doing phenomenal things in our lives as he did with the paralyzed man. All he asks of us is to have faith.

When was a time you doubted God, and why did you doubt him?

_____

_____

_____

_____

How has God answered past doubt in your life, and what did you gain as a result?

_____

_____

_____

_____

Dear God,

You are a God capable of doing far more than I could ever ask for or imagine. Nothing of this earth can ever compare to your goodness, and I confess that I'm not always the best at seeing you for your greatness. Everything is possible when I believe in you, so I ask you to show me where my unbelief prevents me from being in awe of your goodness. Thank you for being a God of amazing grace and for freely extending that grace to me at all times. I ask for your guidance and strength as I continue down the path you have for me, and I pray against anything trying to hinder the next step of that path. Your ways and your thoughts are higher than mine, and although I may not always understand them, I can rest in knowing that your ways are good. Even in my suffering, you are faithful and just to provide. Thank you for everything you have already provided for me and for helping me to show those around me that you are a marvelous God.

In Jesus' name,
Amen.

Chapter Three

GOD IS KIND

Lesson 1: Sympathy

The world we live in has a strong love/hate relationship with kindness. As soon as kids are old enough to grasp the concept of kindness, we teach them to value it. We tell them not to steal toys, not to hit their siblings, and not to say rude things about people. We teach these things as an example of how to show kindness to others, because we all want people to be kind and to show kindness to us. That's all good, but, unfortunately, our world still often lacks in kindness.

If we all want people to be kind to us, and we see kindness as so important that we teach even the youngest children to value it, then why don't we see more kindness in our world? Simply put, our human nature isn't very kind. We teach kids to be kind but often don't demonstrate kindness ourselves.

It's easy for us to come up with reasons why someone doesn't deserve our kindness—maybe they ruined something valuable to us, or they were being discriminatory to a friend of ours. There are plenty of reasons out there for us to justify not being kind to someone, but the important question is this: Where does choosing not to be kind really get us? By not showing kindness, what benefit do we receive other than gratifying our own selfishness and pride?

When was a time that you struggled with being kind to someone else? What was the reason for your struggle?

_____

_____

_____

_____

When was a time someone else showed you kindness, and how did it make you feel?

_____

_____

_____

_____

When was a time that someone else _did not_ show you kindness, and how did it make you feel?

_____

_____

_____

_____

We all know that being kind has benefits, or we wouldn't want people to be kind to us. How do we show kindness and what benefits come from being kind?

Kind: _adjective_ of a sympathetic, forbearing, or pleasant nature; arising from sympathy or forbearance[14]

Unlike the sympathetic nature of kindness, our human nature is selfish. Showing kindness and being sympathetic requires us to look outside of ourselves and into the interests and needs of others. In the self-consumed world we live in,

---

14 _Merriam-Webster's Dictionary and Thesaurus,_ Updated Edition, s.v. "Kind."

this type of culture can be hard to come by. Thankfully, we have a God who sets the example for us and shows sympathy in his nature.

> *For we do not have a high priest who is unable to sympathize with our weaknesses, but one who in every respect has been tempted as we are, yet without sin.* Hebrews 4:15 ESV

That passage tells us how God sympathizes with our weaknesses. Why is that such a big deal? It's a big deal because God has *no obligation* to be sympathetic toward us, yet he still shows us sympathy. Just as we all face temptations, Jesus too was tempted while he lived on this earth; unlike us, however, he resisted those temptations without sinning.

If Jesus acted in the same ways as many in our world do, he would look at all of us who fall victim to the same kinds of temptations that he successfully resisted and would consider himself as "better" than we are. But Jesus doesn't look at us in this way—instead, he is kind and sympathizes with us. Why does Jesus choose to show us kindness and sympathy rather than looking at us as "less than?"

> **Sympathy:** *noun* a relationship between persons or things wherein whatever affects one similarly affects another[15]

The key to God's sympathetic nature comes in the first two words of that definition—God wants a *relationship* with us. In order to show sympathy to someone, a relationship must first exist. Note that this definition doesn't specify the depth of that relationship, meaning that showing sympathy to people should not be conditional to how well we know them or how much we love them. We do not need to be best friends with people before we show them sympathy; we simply need to be more mindful of how certain things affect different people.

How have you seen God's sympathetic nature in your own life?

_____

_____

_____

_____

---

15 *Merriam-Webster's Dictionary and Thesaurus,* Updated Edition, s.v. "Sympathy."

It was the sympathetic nature of God that freed me from the stronghold of needing to drink to hide from feelings of ugliness and disgust for myself. Unlike our world, which expects us to "get over" things after a while, God never expected me to get over anything. Instead, he sat with me, allowed me to feel what I needed to feel, and then responded by reminding me that in his eyes, I am and always have been beautiful.

I didn't fully understand how God could see me as beautiful, but I wanted to understand, so I kept pursuing a relationship with him. The more I pursued seeking a relationship with God, the less I turned to earthly sources like drinking for help.

Just as God displays his value for kindness in the form of seeking a relationship with us, he calls us to have the same mindset in our relationships with others.

> In your relationships with one another, have the same mindset as Christ Jesus: Who, being in very nature God, did not consider equality with God something to be used to his own advantage; rather, he made himself nothing by taking the very nature of a servant, being made in human likeness. And being found in appearance as a man, he humbled himself by becoming obedient to death—even death on a cross! Philippians 2:5–8 NIV

Jesus didn't sin, yet he still sympathizes with us in our sin by taking on the death we all owe for our sin onto himself. Jesus didn't have to let the payment we owe for our sin affect him, but he took it on anyway because of his kindness. He could have used his equality with God to his advantage. Instead, he made himself nothing and died because he is sympathetic and because whatever affects us similarly affects him.

I knew I was far from the only woman who struggled to see myself as beautiful, so as God freed me from the pain that struggle once caused me, a desire to use my newfound freedom as a light to other women was born. I became much more intentional in my relationships and got involved in things like women's ministry groups. Becoming sympathetic becomes a lot more like second nature after knowing great pain and the effects of that pain. Being freed from that pain, I never wanted another woman to be stuck in that kind of pain.

None of us knows great pain better than Jesus does. Jesus understands and sympathizes with us regardless of the depth of our pain. He knows exactly what any pain we will ever deal with feels like, and he is kind enough to sit with us all while we walk through it and heal from it.

What is a way that you can apply the kind of mindset Jesus has in your relationships?

_____

_____

_____

_____

Who is someone to whom you need to show more sympathy, and why?

_____

_____

_____

_____

Lesson 2: Forbearance

The world generally accepts the Golden Rule as a good principle to live by, regardless of one's belief system. Although the word *kind* isn't directly stated in the Golden Rule, we all want to be treated kindly—implying that we cannot "treat others as we want to be treated" unless we treat them with kindness. We all want to live in a society full of kindness. For the most part, we are upset if we see someone being unkind to someone else for no reason. We all know that unkind things take place all over the world each day, and it never seems to end. Why aren't more people getting *upset*?

On one hand, a lack of kindness upsets us; on the other hand, our world quickly justifies unkind actions. Our world loves to place judgment both on and in people, and it will jump at any opportunity available to justify why a person or group of people deserves unkind treatment.

Have you ever intervened in a situation in which someone was being unkind to someone else? If so, what was the result? If not, why did you not intervene?

_____

_____

_____

_____

You, therefore, have no excuse, you who pass judgment on someone else, for at whatever point you judge another, you are condemning yourself, because you who pass judgment do the same things. Now we know that God's judgment against those who do such things is based on truth. So when you, a mere human being, pass judgment on them and yet do the same things, do you think you will escape God's judgment? Or do you show contempt for the riches of his kindness, forbearance and patience, not realizing that God's kindness is intended to lead you to repentance? Romans 2:1–4 NIV

By making the judgment that someone deserves unkind treatment, we give ourselves a reason to look at or think more highly of ourselves. We separate ourselves from those on whom we place judgment, and then we put them in a box based on those judgments. Looking at my life from a worldly context, it would be really easy to justify treating the man who raped me unkindly. He took something from me that I could never get back, so it's only fair for him to feel some pain from someone else's unkind actions toward him, right? As easily "justifiable" as it may seem to be unkind to him in return, where would doing something unkind back to him get me? Not very far, that's where.

I'm not saying he shouldn't be held accountable for his own actions and that he shouldn't see justice for the things he did to me. Sadly, our justice system has a long way to go in properly holding abusers accountable for their actions. What I am saying is that me being unkind to him in return does *nothing* to solve my pain, bring healing, or do any good. What it *does* do is give me actions for which I would also need to be held accountable!

That passage in Romans tells us that none of us is actually "separate" or "in a different box" than any other human. When Paul states in those verses that we "do the same things," he doesn't suggest that we all live the same life. We each live very different lives, but one thing we all do the same is sin. Our sinful nature manifests itself differently in each of us, but none of us is any less guilty of sin than another, and none of us is any more or less deserving of kindness than another.

In reality, there is no reason for God to allow us to escape his judgment of our sin, and yet he gives us a way to escape anyway out of his kindness and *forbearance*. When we repent our sins to God, his kindness prevails every single time.

Describe a time when you found yourself passing judgment on someone. What impact did that judgment have on your relationship with that person?

_____

_____

_____

_____

Has God's kindness ever led you to repentance? If so, what was the result?

_____

_____

_____

_____

> **Forbearance:** *noun* a refraining from the enforcement of something (such as a debt, right, or obligation) that is due[16]

Our human nature does not possess forbearance or the kindness that results from forbearance, but God's nature does, and he offers us his kindness and forbearance as the fruit of his Spirit.

> *But the fruit of the Spirit is love, joy, peace, forbearance, kindness, goodness, faithfulness, gentleness and self-control. Against such things there is no law. Those who belong to Christ Jesus have crucified the*

---

16   *Merriam-Webster.com*, s.v. "Forbearance," accessed December 04, 2022, https://www. merriam-webster.com/

flesh with its passions and desires. Since we live by the Spirit, let us
keep in step with the Spirit. Galatians 5:22–25 NIV

Why should we bother living a life of forbearance and kindness? There is no law against kindness and forbearance, and both are in line with God's heart.

All of the benefits of showing these qualities sound great, so why don't we see more of them? Living a life of kindness and forbearance comes at the cost of putting to death the passions and desires of our flesh. Putting the desires of our flesh aside proves very difficult, but the fruit that comes from putting those desires aside makes crucifying those desires of our flesh worth it every time.

Being a light to others who have been through abuse is a calling that God placed on my life. It would be years before I truly knew how this calling would play out in my life, but something I did know early on is that being a light to other survivors would be impossible if I kept my focus on how to "get back at" the man who abused me.

In order to be that light, I had to show forbearance in the sense of what I thought he deserved, or was due in return, for his actions. In the context of our human nature, showing this forbearance was impossible. The pain I felt was real, and nothing about my pain was "fun" or "enjoyable." Wanting him to feel a similar pain is the natural human response. While wanting him to experience similar feelings is totally justifiable in our world's eyes, putting my energy into those feelings would accomplish nothing in being a light and bringing hope to other survivors.

I was not strong enough on my own to show this kind of forbearance. In reality, none of us can do that in our own strength. When surrendering the desires of the flesh seems impossible, we have a God who overflows with kindness and wants to receive our confessions and repentance with love at all times. It is *never* too late to turn to God and allow him to work in our lives!

What do you think it means to "keep in step with the Spirit"?

_____

_____

_____

_____

What fruit have you seen produced in your life as a result of kindness?

_____

_____

_____

_____

~∽

Lesson 3: Pleasant

Of the many ways we can show kindness, the type of kindness we will address in this lesson is among the most sought after and the easiest to fake. We all want to live a life full of happiness and joy; to fulfill those desires, we seek out that which is *pleasurable* to us.

> **Pleasure:** *noun* a feeling of happy satisfaction and enjoyment[17]

Our world is addicted to seeking pleasure and the feelings of happy satisfaction and enjoyment that come from pleasure. While having pleasure or being pleased by something is not a bad thing, we need to be mindful of the source of that pleasure. I said this type of kindness is among the easiest to fake, because plenty of things in our world come off as pleasing. Those things that give pleasure do not always come from a place of kindness—even *sin* can seem pleasurable!

> *By faith Moses, when he had grown up, refused to be known as the son of Pharaoh's daughter. He chose to be mistreated along with the people of God rather than to enjoy the fleeting pleasures of sin. Hebrews 11:24–25 NIV*

Look again at the definition of *kind*. It describes *kind* as, "of a sympathetic, forbearing, or pleasant nature." With that definition in mind, we see that simply being pleasant isn't enough. To be kind, one must have a pleasant *nature*. The pleasure that comes from sin is *fleeting* and fades. This pleasure from sin is only pleasing in a worldly context; in God's eyes, nothing pleasing comes from sin.

> *Those who obey their human nature cannot please God. Romans 8:8*

---

17 *Merriam-Webster's Dictionary and Thesaurus,* Updated Edition, s.v. "Pleasure."

Do you think it matters if we live a life pleasing to God? Why or why not?

_____

_____

_____

_____

Our sinful human nature is not kind or pleasant, but God's nature is, and God invites each of us to transform our mindset into one that knows kindness.

> *Do not conform to the pattern of this world, but be transformed by the renewing of your mind. Then you will be able to test and approve what God's will is—his good, pleasing and perfect will. Romans 12:2 NIV*

When was a time that you conformed to a standard of this world? What was the result?

_____

_____

_____

_____

Contrary to our human nature, the will of God is pleasing. If we allow God to transform our minds, we can access another aspect of his kindness. In order to live fully in the calling that God placed on my life, I had to transform my mind from being a place that saw myself as disgusting and useless into one that saw myself as beautiful and purposeful. This transformation was imperative if I wanted to live out God's will for my life by being a light to other survivors. How could I confidently tell other survivors they were beautiful regardless of their trauma if I couldn't see myself as beautiful first?

The transformation and renewing of my mind took the better part of two years, but by God's grace and kindness that transformation happened. Seeking this transformation wasn't easy. While seeing myself as unclean wasn't life-giving by any means, it was "safe." Transforming my mind to see myself with anything other than disgust would require the surrendering of what I felt to be true of myself and required me to open up pain from wounds I kept hidden so that they could be healed. From a worldly sense, removing myself from that self-perceived safety and reopening those wounds may not make sense, but what about God's kindness makes doing so worth it? The following passage gives us a glimpse of God's will and the kindness that results from his will in action:

> *"Do not be afraid, little flock, for your Father has been pleased to give you the kingdom. Sell your possessions and give to the poor. Provide purses for yourselves that will not wear out, a treasure in heaven that will never fail, where no thief comes near and no moth destroys. For where your treasure is, there your heart will be also." Luke 12:32–34 NIV*

What do you think Jesus cautions us about when he says, "for where your treasure is, there your heart will be also"?

_____

_____

_____

_____

Jesus shows us here that out of God's pleasant and kind nature, he gives us his kingdom. God doesn't extend this kindness to us for no reason. He loves us more than any of us can fathom, and having us in his kingdom *pleases* him and gives him feelings of joy. To our consumeristic world, selling our possessions and giving to the poor aren't top of mind, but Jesus assures us here that we are not to let fear get in our way of having a giving spirit.

After those two years of transforming my mind and seeking God's will, God gave me my own opportunity to "sell my possessions" so I could live out his will. My senior year of college was coming to an end, and while changing my major midway through college caused me to have to take a victory lap and study for a fifth year to complete my degree, I needed to start figuring out what to do post-graduation. I knew I wanted to continue education and go to graduate school. But where should I go? I had no clue other than the fact that I didn't want to stay in Ohio. So, what did I do? I looked up the top cities in the United States for people in their twenties, I started applying to schools in cities on that list, and I asked God to show me where to go.

A few months later, I got accepted into the University of Utah's MBA program. While having an open door was exciting, I still had some apprehension, so I told myself I wasn't going to accept the offer until I had a chance to check the school out in person and hear from other schools. Soon after, the school hosted an event where they flew in prospective students for a preview weekend, and I found myself heading to Salt Lake City. That weekend I found out that they gave me a scholarship—the school thought they told me about the scholarship months earlier. On top of that, the first day after returning home, I found out that I didn't get into the other school I interviewed with. God continued to make it clear to me that I needed to go to Utah, but would moving 1,600 miles away to a place where I knew no one be worth it?

If I relied on myself to provide for all my needs, the answer would have been "probably not." However, when we involve God, we have nothing to fear, and we can rest in the fact that he provides all of our needs. I didn't need to know why God wanted me to go to Utah. I just needed to know that he wanted me to go there, and I could trust him to take care of the rest.

God extends his kindness to all and freely gives us his kingdom, but it's up to us to make the choice to receive that gift. The pleasures of sin are fleeting, but the kingdom of God and the treasures in it cannot be destroyed. In a culture that loves instant gratification, the immediate but fleeting pleasure of sin comes across as very tempting. Rather than submit to sin's temptation, we have the opportunity to be people who live with a transformed mind that focuses on kindness and invests in a God and a kingdom that never fades.

Are you investing in treasures in heaven? If so, how? If not, what all are you investing in?

_____

_____

_____

_____

Have you seen your mind transformed by God? If so, how has it allowed you to have a more pleasing nature?

_____

_____

_____

_____

Lesson 4: Compassion

When looking to gain understanding on a topic, learning about what that thing *isn't* is just as valuable as learning what it *is*. Because we have spent the first few lessons of this chapter exploring the kindness of God's sympathetic, forbearing, and pleasant nature, we're now going to take a look at what kindness isn't.

> *Get rid of all bitterness, rage and anger, brawling and slander, along with every form of malice. Be kind and compassionate to one another, forgiving each other, just as in Christ God forgave you.*
> *Ephesians 4:31–32 NIV*

This passage calls us to be kind to one another, but first, it instructs us to rid our lives of all bitterness, rage, anger, brawling, slander, and malice. Easy enough, right? Of course not—our world is full of every single one of these qualities. At some point in our lives, we've all been guilty of not getting rid of those qualities, and as a result did something that wasn't kind. I don't say that to make you feel like a terrible person; it simply means that you're not God.

What prevents you from getting rid of all of the bitterness, rage, anger, brawling, slander, or malice in your life?

_____

_____

_____

_____

Before talking more about God's kindness, it's important to note that God does indeed have anger too. However, we cannot use the fact that God experiences anger to disprove his kindness—human anger does not have the same effect as God's anger.

> My dear brothers and sisters, take note of this: Everyone should be quick to listen, slow to speak and slow to become angry, because human anger does not produce the righteousness that God desires. James 1:19–20 NIV
>
> "In your anger do not sin": Do not let the sun go down while you are still angry, and do not give the devil a foothold. Ephesians 4:26–27 NIV

It is possible to have anger and not sin, but our human anger does not produce the righteousness God desires, so we are told to get rid of it.

What about human anger do you think is opposed to the righteousness God desires?

_____

_____

_____

_____

Human anger does not produce the righteousness God desires, but kindness does produce righteousness, and God instructs us to show that kindness through compassion. Compassion can be hard to come by in a world stuck in cycles of anger, bitterness, and rage. God sets the tone for us in showing compassion as seen in this chapter of the Bible, which is appropriately titled *The Compassion of the LORD.*

> "Come, everyone who thirsts, come to the waters; and he who has no money, come, buy and eat! Come, buy wine and milk without money and without price. Why do you spend your money for that which is not bread, and your labor for that which does not satisfy? Listen diligently to me, and eat what is good, and delight yourselves in rich food." Isaiah 55:1–2 ESV

Do you go to God when you lack something? Why or why not?

_____

_____

_____

_____

We can read those verses and think they don't apply to us when we live in a world where for many, food and water are easily accessible. However, when Jesus refers to himself as the "bread of life," he isn't referring to the kind of bread we make sandwiches with; instead, he is speaking of bread in a spiritual sense.

> _"For the bread of God is he who comes down from heaven and gives life to the world." They said to him, "Sir, give us this bread always." Jesus said to them, "I am the bread of life; whoever comes to me shall not hunger, and whoever believes in me shall never thirst." John 6:33–35 ESV_

Out of his kind and compassionate nature, God presents us with this opportunity to never again go hungry or be thirsty. This invitation to receive God's compassion is one that is available to everyone. When we remain in sin, we live a life of hunger, unfulfilled and always wanting more. When we believe in Jesus and receive his compassion on us and forgiveness of our sin, we become filled.

Spiritually speaking, moving out to Utah tested whether or not I would allow God to fill me. I knew God was real, and I saw him at work in my life. I saw his provision and goodness first-hand, but I hadn't really allowed myself to become _dependent_ on God to fulfill me to the point where I didn't hunger and thirst for other earthly things.

A good portion of my faith still depended on the faith of the people around me, because I hadn't made my faith my own. Being removed from the people and the church I had grown to love forced me to have to turn to God for my needs and fulfillment in a way that I never before needed to do. Although at the time I wouldn't have told you that I depended on other people's faith, I can look back now and see otherwise. In order to experience that reality, I needed to experience spiritual hunger without any sources of fulfillment other than Jesus, and he was kind enough to stay by my side in Utah just as he did in Ohio.

No amount of money or good deeds will ever make us more worthy to receive God's compassion. In both the John and Isaiah passages, we are invited to "come." We aren't told *when* to come, and we aren't told *how*; we're simply told that once we do, hunger and thirst will be no more!

Why is it so significant that Jesus declared we will never hunger or thirst if we both come to and believe him?

_____

_____

_____

_____

Have you accepted Jesus's invitation to come? Why or why not?

_____

_____

_____

_____

Dear God,

Your kindness is a natural response to your sympathetic, forbearing, and pleasant nature. Unlike other gods, you sympathize with my weaknesses, because you have been tempted in every way and you overcame those temptations without sin. Thank you for being a God who wants a relationship with me so badly that you willingly show kindness to me, even though I have gone against your will. I confess that at times, instead of showing kindness, I pass judgment to others even though I am just as guilty of sin as they are. Kindness is a fruit of your Spirit, and with the power of your Spirit, I am able to show kindness to others in all circumstances. Help me to renew and transform my mind to focus on your pleasing will for my life rather than give in to the fleeting pleasures of sin. You are the bread of life and by your kindness you offer me everything I need to live a fulfilled life.

In Jesus' name,
Amen.

Chapter Four

GOD IS FREEDOM

Lesson 1: Independence

The United States has famously earned the nickname, "the land of the free." To establish independence from Great Britain, our founding fathers wrote the Declaration of Independence and signed it on July 4, 1776. Every year on July 4, the United States celebrates its freedom on a holiday better known as Independence Day.

We all have a desire for freedom, and people from all over the world move to the United States in search of obtaining the freedom it offers. Why would people drop everything they have to move halfway around the world just to find and establish freedom? What is it that makes freedom such a big deal?

Freedom: *noun* the quality or state of being free: independence; exemption, release; ease, facility; the ability or capacity to act without undue hindrance or restraint[18]

While I can't say that I have fled to a new place in search of personal rights or freedoms, moving across the country was my own search for a different kind of freedom. I couldn't tell you what kind of freedom I was looking for at the time; I just knew I wasn't content in my current location, and something

---

18   *Merriam-Webster's Dictionary and Thesaurus,* Updated Edition, s.v. "Freedom."

needed to change. I saw graduate school as an open door to explore a new area. At the very worst, I could move back to Ohio after those two years of school were over if I didn't like my new area. Someone in the business world might say that the opportunity cost of moving to a new city for graduate school was a low one to pay.

In our own unique way, we all sacrifice something in our lives as a response to our desire for freedom, whether that freedom be financial, career-based, religious, or some other form. We are not alone in having this desire; God also shares in our desire for freedom. He wants us to live as free people, and he provides the way for us to receive that freedom.

> *Freedom is what we have—Christ has set us free! Stand, then, as*
> *free people, and do not allow yourselves to become slaves again.*
> *Galatians 5:1*

God sacrificed his only Son's life to give us freedom. The question is, what does that sacrifice free us from? In the first definition of *freedom,* we see reference to the word *independence* again.

Independent: *adjective* not subject to control by others[19]

Where do you wish you had more independence in your life and why?

_____

_____

_____

_____

For us to have independence, we must be freed from the *control* of something or someone. Ask anyone who has known me well from an early age—they will tell you that I've always been an independent person and I don't take well to anyone who tries to control any part of my life. I'm a rebel at heart, and when someone tells me I can't do something, it often provides fuel for me to want to prove them wrong.

---

19   *Merriam-Webster's Dictionary and Thesaurus,* Updated Edition, s.v. "Independent."

Going to graduate school was no different. Not everyone around me responded well to my wanting to move across the country and pursue something completely different from my undergraduate degree in chemistry. Some tried to convince me to stay, suggesting I get a job and use my degree for a couple of years before going back to school, but deep down I knew that wasn't what I wanted.

Whether it be the media, our jobs, school, or something else, many different things in this world attempt to control our lives. With worldly things such as our jobs, school, and the media, we have the ability to decide whether we allow them to have control in our lives. However, is there something else that we *cannot* free ourselves from the control of? If God is a God of freedom in his nature, that would suggest that we are subject to the control of something that God can provide us independence from.

> *In the same way, count yourselves dead to sin but alive to God in Christ Jesus. Therefore do not let sin reign in your mortal body so that you obey its evil desires. Do not offer any part of yourself to sin as an instrument of wickedness, but rather offer yourselves to God as those who have been brought from death to life; and offer every part of yourself to him as an instrument of righteousness. For sin shall no longer be your master, because you are not under the law, but under grace.*
> *Romans 6:11–14 NIV*

Those who wrote the Declaration of Independence wrote it to be free from Great Britain. God on the other hand, gives us freedom and independence from the control of our *sin*.

What does the fact that God wants to free you from the control of your sin tell you about his character?

_____

_____

_____

_____

How has God freed you from the control of your sin?

_____

_____

_____

_____

Why do we need God to free us from the control of our sin? Later on in the same chapter, Paul provides us with the answer:

> For the wages of sin is death, but the gift of God is eternal life in Christ
> Jesus our Lord. Romans 6:23 NIV

If we stay under sin's control and pay its wage of death ourselves, we receive eternal separation from God. God loves us too much to remain eternally separated from us, so he sent Jesus to pay the wage for our sin. Out of _grace_, God frees us from sin's control, and by doing so, he also gives us independence from paying sin's wage of death.

This kind of freedom—freedom from paying the wage for our sins—can _only_ be found by placing our faith in Jesus and receiving his death to cover what we can't pay. As soon as we accept Jesus as our Savior, access to the freedom we all want is ours. What does this freedom allow us to do?

> For you were called to freedom, brothers. Only do not use your freedom
> as an opportunity for the flesh, but through love serve one another.
> Galatians 5:13 ESV

God never gifts us anything with the intention of having the gift benefit only ourselves. When we accept freedom from the control of our sin that he gifts us, we can then use our gift to love and serve those around us. Loving and serving those around us is the best way to show others what the freedom God offers looks like. We cannot love and serve those around us _and_ be under the control of our sin at the same time.

What do you think Paul means when he says not to use our freedom as an opportunity for the flesh?

_____

_____

_____

_____

How can you serve someone in your life right now and point them to the freedom found in Christ?

_____

_____

_____

_____

~⌒

Lesson 2: Exemption

Exam week in high school was always one of my favorites—and no, it's not because I enjoy taking exams. Quite the opposite. Exam week was one of my favorites because at my high school, if we received *A*s both quarters of a semester in any class, we received an *exemption* from the final exam for that class. With this rule in place, the only exam I usually took was English. (I know, that's likely not what you expected to hear from someone who writes books.)

Since I wasn't required to take the rest of my exams, I was *freed* from going to school during the allotted exam times—what teenager doesn't love an almost six-day weekend?

Exempt: *adjective* free from the liability to which others are subject[20]

The word *exemption* appears in the definition for *freedom*, but how does exemption provide freedom?

---

[20] *Merriam-Webster's Dictionary and Thesaurus,* Updated Edition, s.v. "Exempt."

Unlike the previous lesson where freedom came from being freed from control, freedom through exemption comes by no longer being subject to a liability. If we apply this concept to my exam week, exams were the liability, and getting good grades freed, or exempted, me from taking on that liability.

When have you been exempted from a liability, and what freedom did you obtain as a result?

_____

_____

_____

_____

By moving across the country for graduate school, I removed myself from many earthly liabilities I previously had. I no longer lived near my family, my friends, or the church I attended. I was now physically unable to attend all the events I normally would have attended. With having all of this newfound ease of earthly liabilities, I had a lot more time to spend with God than I would otherwise have had.

On one hand, I fully believe that God always keeps our best interest in mind and would never ask us to do something if it wasn't for our good. On the other hand, I would be lying if I said the dramatic change in my life that resulted from the move wasn't painful in some respects. It wasn't painful because God made it painful; it was painful because it forced me to confront my humanness on a deeper level. I was no longer surrounded every day by people who knew me deeply and loved me. Instead, I had to rely on God and his love for me more than ever before.

Spiritually speaking, I still desired to be known and loved—we all share these desires. Often times, we place the liability of the desires to be known and loved onto the world. The problem with this mentality is that anything that is of this world will only free us, or give us ease, from our desires to be known and loved *temporarily*. God is the only source able to permanently ease us from our desire to be loved. We see a display of that love in this passage about exemption:

After Jesus and his disciples arrived in Capernaum, the collectors of the two-drachma temple tax came to Peter and asked, "Doesn't your teacher pay the temple tax?" "Yes, he does," he replied. When Peter came into the house, Jesus was the first to speak. "What do you think, Simon?" he asked. "From whom do the kings of the earth collect duty and taxes—from their own children or from others?" "From others," Peter answered. "Then the children are exempt," Jesus said to him. "But so that we may not cause offense, go to the lake and throw out your line. Take the first fish you catch; open its mouth and you will find a four-drachma coin. Take it and give it to them for my tax and yours." Matthew 17:24–27 NIV

In this passage, Peter and Jesus came across the liability of paying a temple tax. Jesus explains to Peter how to gain exemption from paying the temple tax. What was the exemption? Being a *child* of the one collecting the tax. Notice that right after Jesus points out that children receive exemption from paying the two-drachma temple tax, he tells Peter to throw out his line and open the mouth of the first fish he catches. What does Peter find in that fish? Peter finds a four-drachma coin.

By Peter acting on his faith in Jesus and casting out the line, Jesus provided a way to cover *both* of their two-drachma temple tax payments. Through this provision, Jesus treats Peter as one of his children, making it so Peter didn't have to come up with the temple tax payment himself.

God wants to treat us like his children just as he did with Peter in that passage. Becoming a child of God requires us to put our faith in him and be born again with his Spirit. Why is it important for us to believe in God, be born again, and become his child? It's important because we *all* have a liability to pay.

For God loved the world so much that he gave his only Son, so that everyone who believes in him may not die but have eternal life. For God did not send his Son into the world to be its judge, but to be its savior. John 3:16–17

The liability we owe is death. God wants to give us *all* an exemption from our liability, so he sent Jesus to die in our place. By believing in Jesus and receiving his death on our behalf, we are free from owing the death to which we subjected ourselves. In exchange for the death we once owed, we become a child of God and receive eternal life.

Why do you think John makes a point of saying that God didn't send Jesus to be the world's judge, but rather its savior?

_____

_____

_____

_____

Just like kings today have kingdoms on earth, God's kingdom is heaven, and all who are a child of God get to enter God's kingdom. God is a good father. He _wants_ us to be free, and it's out of his great love for us that he makes our freedom possible.

What does being a child of God mean to you?

_____

_____

_____

_____

Has the freedom found in Christ allowed you to draw nearer to God? If so, how?

_____

_____

_____

_____

～

Lesson 3: Ease

I was the kind of student many people hated in school. Why? For the most part, school came easily to me. My *ease* in school gave me access to certain freedoms that others didn't have—freedom from spending a lot of time studying and freedom from worrying about upcoming tests.

We all want the freedom that comes from having ease. This kind of freedom often proves difficult to come by because we often focus on the hardship in our world. I'm sure we've all heard someone say something like, "No one ever promised that life would be easy."

Although it is true that hardship exists in this world—and that hardship in this world won't go away until heaven and earth are restored—I believe that we often make life on earth harder than it needs to be because we don't involve God enough in our lives. Freedom is in the heart of who God is, and part of that freedom includes having *ease*. If we find our life in the things of this world, that life won't be easy—or freeing.

How have you experienced freedom from being at ease in a situation? What allowed you to be at ease?

_____

_____

_____

_____

Our world can't promise us that we will be at ease if we listen to what it says, but God can, and he does.

> *"For the waywardness of the simple will kill them, and the complacency of fools will destroy them; but whoever listens to me will live in safety and be at ease, without fear of harm." Proverbs 1:32–33 NIV*

Those verses declare that if we listen to God, we can find safety and ease—free from fear and harm. Sounds great, right? Every one of those qualities is part of a life we all want, so why don't we listen to God more often?

Have you ever had a hard time listening to God? If so, why?

_____

_____

_____

_____

Have you found safety or ease from something by listening to God? If so, how?

_____

_____

_____

_____

Personally, I think we don't listen to God more often because we forget the extent of his *goodness*. When God promises us safety and ease, what does he give us freedom from?

Ease: *noun* freedom from pain, discomfort, or concern[21]

By promising us that we will be at ease if we listen to him, God gives us access to freedom from pain, discomfort, and concern. Access to this kind of freedom is a promise *only* God can make. God never contradicts his Word, and his Word tells of how God provides freedom from:

Pain: *"He will wipe away every tear from their eyes, and death shall be no more, neither shall there be mourning, nor crying, nor pain anymore, for the former things have passed away." Revelation 21:4 ESV*

Discomfort: *Even though I walk through the darkest valley, I will fear no evil, for you are with me; your rod and your staff, they comfort me. Psalm 23:4 NIV*

Concern: *"So don't be all upset, always concerned about what you will eat and drink. (For the pagans of this world are always concerned about all these things.) Your Father knows that you need these things.*

---

21 *Merriam-Webster's Dictionary and Thesaurus,* Updated Edition, s.v. "Ease."

Instead, be concerned with his Kingdom, and he will provide you with
these things." Luke 12:29–31

I'm not saying that pain, discomfort, and concern are going to disappear from this world any time soon. We live in a broken world. What I *am* saying is that we have a God who wants to *free* us from those things. What benefit do we receive as a result of this freedom? By being freed from the pain, discomfort, and concerns with which this world confronts us, we become free to take steps of faith into God's calling on our life.

Being a survivor of sexual assault is by far the deepest pain I've endured, the darkest valley I've walked through, and the most concerned I've ever been with what people thought about me. The only reason I took a step of faith to move away from everything I knew to pursue a greater calling on my life is because during the two and a half years between the night of the assault and the day I moved, God progressively gave me ease from that pain. He sat beside me in all those sleepless nights wiping away my tears, giving me comfort in knowing that pain would not have the final say in my life, and freeing me from the concerns of people's opinions about me.

I had big aspirations to lead a weekly women's Bible study at my house in Utah similar to the ones I had attended in Ohio. Just a couple of months after moving to Utah, God opened up a door; it was the first step that enabled me to start giving back to other women. Upon partnering with other women who were already in Utah, we started a monthly women's event where we invited a different guest speaker each month to address a different attribute of being a godly woman. While this wasn't something I personally spoke at, it did provide a great opportunity to make a lot of valuable connections and network with like-minded people in my new setting.

Because God is a God of freedom, he provides us with our every need, always comforts us, and gives us the opportunity to spend eternity with him in heaven free of pain. While all of the freedom and ease God gave me from those hardships provided great benefit to my life, God doesn't ever bless us with the intent of us keeping that benefit for ourselves. God made it known very quickly to me in my new environment that I was far from alone in my concerns for his kingdom and desires to bring his freedom to this world. While making a move across the country could have easily been an extremely isolating experience, God provided a community of support that started making my dreams become a reality.

What pain, discomfort, or concern is in your life right now that is causing you to feel a lack of freedom? How can you ask God to intervene?

_____

_____

_____

_____

What do you think Jesus means when he says we should "be concerned for God's kingdom," and how can you show that concern?

_____

_____

_____

_____

∾

Lesson 4: Hindrance

We live in a very busy world. We all have commitments, and those commitments come with a set of expectations that involve both our time and energy. Some of our commitments are ones we choose to make, while others aren't. Chances are, we've all found ourselves at some point in life wanting more *freedom* over our schedule. This kind of freedom is described as "the ability or capacity to act without undue hindrance or restraint."[22]

If we had complete freedom of our schedule and could act without hindrances, all of our calendars would look different. This freedom from hindrance applies to more than just our daily schedules, but also to our relationship with God.

> *From that time Jesus began to show his disciples that he must go to Jerusalem and suffer many things from the elders and chief priests and scribes, and be killed, and on the third day be raised. And Peter took*

---

22 *Merriam-Webster's Dictionary and Thesaurus,* Updated Edition, s.v. "Freedom."

him aside and began to rebuke him, saying, "Far be it from you, Lord! This shall never happen to you." But he turned and said to Peter, "Get behind me, Satan! You are a hindrance to me. For you are not setting your mind on the things of God, but on the things of man." Matthew 16:21–23 ESV

I moved to Utah as an act of faith in *where* God wanted me to be. (To be quite honest, it didn't require a lot of faith, because I didn't care where I went as long as the "where" wasn't Ohio.) I did not move to Utah in an act of faith about *what* God wanted me to do. I had my mind made up that no matter where I moved, I was moving to go to graduate school. The decision to go to graduate school created a lot of hindrance in my schedule when it came to serving in church and growing my relationship with God.

Graduate school came with a schedule that changed every three to four months, with classes at all times of the day. Additionally, I had to work around multiple other people's schedules as part of numerous group projects assigned. Making my schedule at school a priority put my schedule with God on the backburner. I fit time in with him whenever it was convenient for me and after all else was taken care of.

This mindset is far from the mindset that Jesus took in that passage in Matthew. Jesus came to earth for a specific purpose, and nothing hindered him from accomplishing that purpose. The passage starts out with Jesus explaining to his disciples the plan God had for Jesus to die for our sins. Peter immediately tries to bring a hindrance to that plan. In his response, Jesus brings light to Peter's hindrance. Jesus calls Satan out and says that the mindset behind Peter's comment to Jesus was a mindset of man rather than the mindset of God.

What hinders you from keeping your mind set on the things of God?

_____

_____

_____

_____

What happens when we keep our mind set on the things of man and not of God? Paul describes the results of both mindsets in his letter to the Romans:

Those who live according to the flesh have their minds set on what the flesh desires; but those who live in accordance with the Spirit have their minds set on what the Spirit desires. The mind governed by the flesh is death, but the mind governed by the Spirit is life and peace. Romans 8:5–6 NIV

How have you seen a difference in these two mindsets in your own life?

_____

_____

_____

_____

Living in a mindset ruled by our flesh results in death. Our flesh is weak, and Satan does everything he can to both hinder us from living in accordance with the Spirit and keep us operating in our weakness. On the other hand, a mindset governed by God's Spirit brings life and peace. With God's Spirit, we hold the power to overcome that hindrance and find freedom.

Now the Lord is the Spirit, and where the Spirit of the Lord is, there is freedom. 2 Corinthians 3:17 NIV

God's intention from the very beginning of creating mankind was for us to freely be in a relationship with him. Our sin separated us from God and took away that freedom. Jesus dying for our sins brought restoration and gave us back the ability to freely communicate with God. God's Spirit by nature is a Spirit of freedom, and it gives us the freedom to act in the purpose God placed in our lives without restraint. God's Spirit also gives us the ability to communicate with God free from any hindrance.

What was your life like before you prayed to receive God's Spirit? How did you see a lack of freedom in your life?

_____

_____

_____

_____

Have you experienced the freedom that God's Spirit offers? If so, what hindrance did God's Spirit provide you freedom from?

_____

_____

_____

_____

Dear God,

Thank you for being a God who desires for me to have freedom. You sent your Son to sacrifice his life for mine and to free me from sin's control over me. There is nothing I can do to earn freedom from the control of my sin; it is only by your love that I am set free. Your goodness enables me to be free from the fear of pain, discomfort, and concern in this world. You are always right beside me, ready to walk through the troubles I come across in this world. I confess that I don't always make time for you and that I allow things to hinder my relationship with you. Please show me where I am not keeping my eyes fixed on you. My flesh is weak, but your Spirit is strong, and gives me the strength and freedom to live in the purpose that you have given me without restraint.

In Jesus' name,
Amen.

Chapter Five

GOD IS JUST

Lesson 1: Reason

Any time we take an action, we subject ourselves to the outcome or consequence of that action. In physics, this phenomenon is summed up in Newton's Third Law of Motion, which states, "For every action there is an equal and opposite reaction." When we apply actions to physical matter in this world, that matter has no choice but to react. If we apply enough force to an inanimate object, the object moves, because it has no other choice but to move.

Actions that involve other humans aren't quite so black-and-white. There are plenty of actions that happen in our world which continue on without an outcome or consequence. Injustice occurs any time that proper consequences aren't paid. The injustices of our world often leave us feeling unsettled in some way. We know injustice isn't right, but we don't always do something about it. Why is that?

Depending on the type of action taken, justice comes in good and bad contexts. The verse below demonstrates the contrast in the two types of outcomes:

> *When justice is done, it is a joy to the righteous but terror to evildoers.*
> *Proverbs 21:15 ESV*

What do you think the verse means when it says that justice is a "joy to the righteous?"

_____

_____

_____

_____

Unlike the world we live in, God is perfectly just, and he lets no action go unnoticed. Our world does a great job of wanting to see justice served when bringing terror to evildoers, so for the purpose of this chapter, we're going to explore other angles of justice.

> **Just:** *adjective* having basis in or conforming to fact or reason: reasonable; conforming to a standard of correctness; morally or legally right; being what is merited[23]

First, we see a correlation to the words *just* and *reasonable*. If an action is to be considered "just," it must have *reasoning* behind it. Depending on what we aim to accomplish with our actions, we are great at coming up with reasons to "justify" why we do the things we do. Most of the time, that justification comes with selfish motives.

While furthering my education can be seen as a noble accomplishment on one hand, my decision to do so came largely from a selfish place. Instead of asking God what to do with my life after I completed my undergraduate studies, I invited God into *my* agenda. With all of the doors that God opened to make graduate school a reality in my life, it seemed as if he was on board with my plan, which made it even easier for me to both reason with and justify my plan.

In reality, God had a totally different plan for me. What was it? I had no clue, because I didn't have that kind of relationship with God at the time. I was too concerned with the success of my plan, and not concerned enough with talking to God and seeking his plan. Because of this, it took me a few

---

23 *Merriam-Webster's Dictionary and Thesaurus,* Updated Edition, s.v. "Just."

years to figure out just how wrong I was in thinking I knew where my life was heading.

Have you ever invited God to join you in your plan for your life? How did that plan end up?

_____

_____

_____

_____

Our justice system supports this idea that reasoning must exist for something to be just—everyone is innocent until proven guilty. From a worldly standpoint, there was nothing wrong with the approach I took with regard to my life plan. I never feared that I would be "punished" in any way for the decision I made to go graduate school. I had sound reasoning for why I wanted to continue my education and executed my plan based on that reasoning.

God also supports this idea that reasoning must exist for something to be just—he never acts without reason, and he calls us to act in the same way.

> *Do not accuse anyone for no reason—when they have done you no*
> *harm. Proverbs 3:30 NIV*

Have you ever been accused of something you didn't do? What was it, and how did it make you feel?

_____

_____

_____

_____

It's one thing to know that God doesn't do anything without reason, but do we know what reasoning he uses?

"Come now, let us reason together, says the LORD: though your sins are like scarlet, they shall be as white as snow; though they are red like crimson, they shall become like wool. If you are willing and obedient, you shall eat the good of the land; but if you refuse and rebel, you shall be eaten by the sword; for the mouth of the LORD has spoken." Isaiah 1:18–20 ESV

The best part about God's justice comes with the way he reasons. All of us have sinned, and the wage for our sin is death. God, being a just God, cannot let the death owed for our sin go unpaid. God doesn't want us to die and remain separated from him, so rather than forcing us to pay the death we owe, he offered his Son as a sacrifice to die in our place.

Since we have now been justified by his blood, how much more shall we be saved from God's wrath through him! Romans 5:9 NIV

What does it mean that we have been justified by the blood of Jesus? If we take a deeper look at God's reasoning in Isaiah, we see God say that our sins are like scarlet, but they shall *become* white as snow. God is saying here that if things stay as is, our sins make us red like scarlet, but that there is a way we can become white like snow, or pure. As he continues with his reasoning, God provides the answer about how we can achieve this purification: we have to be *willing*.

Willing to do what, exactly? We must be willing to receive Jesus as our Savior. It is *only* by the blood of Jesus that we are justified and free from paying the price for our sin. If we refuse and rebel as mentioned in Isaiah, we subject ourselves to the wrath from which God wants to save us. The essence of God's goodness lies in the fact that he knows we all deserve to die, but instead, he reasons with us and provides a way to receive eternal life.

How is the motive for God's reasoning different from ours?

_____

_____

_____

_____

What does the way in which God reasons say about his heart for justice?

_____

_____

_____

_____

What does being willing or obedient to God look like for you right now?

_____

_____

_____

_____

Lesson 2: Correctness

Even though God created each of us as a unique being, there are some things that I think we all share. We all want to be loved, we all want to know we have a purpose, and we all love being *right*.

Too often, we find our worth in this world based on how "right" we are. We tell ourselves that if we do or get something wrong, then there must also be something wrong with us. The problem with this mentality—besides the fact that it's a lie—is the inconsistent standard on which we base our "wrongness." The lack of a consistent standard for right and wrong in this world results in much of the injustice we see, as the word *just* means "conforming to a standard of correctness."[24]

In order to see uniform justice in this world, everyone would need to conform to the *same* standard. However, we can't conform to just *any* standard; it must be a standard of *correctness*. The question is, what does that standard of correctness look like? Not only do the standards in our world differ from region

---

24 *Merriam-Webster's Dictionary and Thesaurus,* Updated Edition, s.v. "Just."

to region, but they also constantly change. The world will never fully agree on a universal standard of correctness. The good news is that the world doesn't have to come up with a standard to agree on, because God already made the standard for correctness!

> *All Scripture is breathed out by God and profitable for teaching,*
> *for reproof, for correction, and for training in righteousness, that*
> *the man of God may be complete, equipped for every good work.*
> 2 Timothy 3:16–17 ESV

Have you ever used the Bible for correction? If so, how? If not, how do you think it could be used for correction?

_____

_____

_____

_____

There is great significance in the declaration made in these verses. Timothy writes that *all* Scripture is God-breathed and profitable for correction. Think about it—something cannot be useful for correction unless it both knows what the correct way is and can provide the correct way. As the Creator of the world and everything in it, God set the standard for correctness. The standard God set isn't a secret—all we have to do is read the Bible.

Since God already gave us the standard for correctness, why don't we see more justice in our world? As the definition for the word *just* showed, simply *knowing* the standard for correctness isn't enough—we must also *conform* to the standard. If justice only depended on knowing the correct standard, we would see a lot more justice in our world today. Knowing the standard does no good unless we also *adhere* to that standard. Adhering to God's standard requires us to act outside of our human nature, which is uncomfortable.

Have you ever had a hard time conforming to the standards written in the Bible? If so, why?

_____

_____

_____

_____

In order to get to a place in our lives where we want to adhere to God's standard, we must first come to a place of *surrender*. Why? Because at some point, we've all been wrong. We've all wronged God, gone against his standard, and sinned.

As someone who had formed part of my identity on my ability to get right answers for all of my life until it was time to start graduate school, this was all easier said than done. While I was growing up, I was always seen as one of the smart kids in my grade—largely because of my math abilities—and I won numerous awards for those abilities beginning in first grade and continuing through graduate school. I don't share that to brag, but to make the point that being "smart" and "right" became so much a part of who I was known as, that it in turn generated a deeply rooted fear of being seen as "wrong" or "stupid."

This fear of being perceived as wrong or stupid played out in more areas of my life than just academia. One of those other areas was in my relationship with God. Coming to a place where I surrendered to God the fact that I don't always know what's best for my life would be tackling that fear head on. I needed to admit that I wasn't right, and I wasn't ready to do that yet, so I didn't. Instead, I kept that barrier up in my relationship with God, and I know I'm far from alone in doing that.

At some point, we've all put up barriers between us and God because conforming to our own lifestyle was either easier or more comfortable. The standards of our world can be enticing, but they do not always have our best interest in mind.

> *Do not conform yourselves to the standards of this world, but let God transform you inwardly by a complete change of your mind. Then you will be able to know the will of God—what is good and is pleasing to him and is perfect. Romans 12:2*

This verse shows us that we *cannot* conform to the patterns of this world and do the will of God at the same time. In order to not conform to the standards of this world, our minds have to be *transformed*. To obtain this transformation, we need the power of the Holy Spirit.

> *What the Law could not do, because human nature was weak, God did. He condemned sin in human nature by sending his own Son, who came with a nature like our sinful nature, to do away with sin. God did this so that the righteous demands of the Law might be fully satisfied in us who live according to the Spirit, and not according to human nature. Those who live as their human nature tells them to, have their minds controlled by what human nature wants. Those who live as the Spirit tells them to, have their minds controlled by what the Spirit wants. To be controlled by human nature results in death; to be controlled by the Spirit results in life and peace. And so people become enemies of God when they are controlled by their human nature; for they do not obey God's law, and in fact they cannot obey it. Romans 8:3–7*

What is a way that God has either already transformed you or that you would like to be transformed by God?

_____

_____

_____

_____

God's law is the standard of correctness to live by. The problem is, we can't conform to God's standard and live in our human nature. Our human nature is weak. God knows we're too weak to fulfill the Law, but his fully just and loving nature did not allow him to leave the Law unfulfilled, either. God sent Jesus to be the fulfillment of the Law for us and to gift us with the Holy Spirit as a result of his death. Out of this act of justice, God offers us the opportunity to live a life controlled by the Spirit rather than by our human nature. With

God's Spirit, we have the power needed to conform to the only *true* standard of correctness.

How has living according to your human nature resulted in death?

_____

_____

_____

_____

How has living according to the Holy Spirit resulted in life or peace?

_____

_____

_____

_____

Lesson 3: Righteousness

In a matter of a few minutes, each of us could find a different news article that calls out someone's unjust behavior. Chances are, that article would tell us how the actions leading to the unjust behavior were *morally wrong* and what should have been done instead. But how does any publication, analyst, or reporter know what is morally right?

Our behavior is driven in part by our own unique set of morals. Our morals help us determine our view of right and wrong, and they help us act accordingly. For the most part, we act on what we feel is "morally or legally right," or in other words, *just*.[25]

---

25 *Merriam-Webster's Dictionary and Thesaurus,* Updated Edition, s.v. "Just."

What is a moral you hold and how does it influence your behavior?

_____

_____

_____

_____

While we don't see the word *moral* appear often in the Bible, this concept of being morally right comes up numerous times in the form of *righteousness*.

Righteous: *adjective* morally right or justifiable[26]

Although the justice in this world is often questionable at best when it comes to acting on what is morally right, God's righteousness is unchanging and everlasting.

> *Your righteousness is everlasting and your law is true. Psalm 119:142 NIV*

What does an everlasting righteousness say about God's character? It says that he always knows what is morally right, and he always acts justifiably on it. God gave us the rubric for what is morally and legally right when he gave us his law. Unlike God and his everlasting righteousness, none of us will gain righteousness because of the law.

> *What then? Are we Jews any better off? No, not at all. For we have already charged that all, both Jews and Greeks, are under sin, as it is written: "None is righteous, no, not one;" Romans 3:9–10 ESV*

All of us have sinned and gone against what God states as morally right, which means we cannot gain righteousness from the law. The good news for us is, God doesn't *expect* us to gain our righteousness from the law—he knows it's not possible. Our righteousness is found in Jesus alone.

> *"I do not set aside the grace of God, for if righteousness could be gained through the law, Christ died for nothing!" Galatians 2:21 NIV*

Paul makes a bold claim here by saying that if we think we can gain righteousness from our own actions, then Jesus died for nothing. As bold

---

26 *Merriam-Webster.com*, s.v. "Righteous," accessed December 04, 2022, https://www.merriam-webster.com/

as that may be, Paul isn't saying anything new here. Jesus made a similar declaration himself:

> While Jesus was having dinner at Matthew's house, many tax collectors and sinners came and ate with him and his disciples. When the Pharisees saw this, they asked his disciples, "Why does your teacher eat with tax collectors and sinners?" On hearing this, Jesus said, "It is not the healthy who need a doctor, but the sick. But go and learn what this means: 'I desire mercy, not sacrifice.' For I have not come to call the righteous, but sinners." Matthew 9:10–13 NIV

What do you think Jesus means when he says, "I desire mercy, not sacrifice"?

_____

_____

_____

_____

Jesus states that he came to call sinners. Who exactly fits the definition of "a sinner"? Being a sinner simply means "missing the mark," and in this case, the "mark" is God's law. All of us have broken God's law at some point, which means that none of us is righteous. We have all sinned, and that means that we can all answer Jesus's call. The key is that we have to willingly make the choice to answer the call.

In one way or another, we are all "sick" from our sin, and only Jesus can heal us from that sickness. God created each of us to have free will. If we want to receive the healing that Jesus offers for our sickness to sin, we must confront Jesus, answer his call, and confess our sins to him. When we do so, Jesus cleanses us from our unrighteousness.

> If we claim to be without sin, we deceive ourselves and the truth is not in us. If we confess our sins, he is faithful and just and will forgive us our sins and purify us from all unrighteousness. 1 John 1:8–9 NIV

Have you answered Jesus's call? If not, would you like to? If so, what has he said to you?

_____

_____

_____

_____

By saying he hasn't come to call the righteous, Jesus isn't giving us permission to sin as we please. What does it mean to not sin as we please? That depends on who you ask. To the world, as long as we're keeping basic morals like not killing people, stealing, abusing, or discriminating others, we're doing pretty good. To God, it looks a little different. To begin to see those differences, all we have to do is look to the first two commandments of having no other gods above God and not making idols.

As graduate school progressed, the question at the forefront of my and all my classmates' minds was where we would work after graduation. I remained determined to follow my plan for my life and walk down the path of corporate America, so all of my actions responded accordingly. I spent hours perfecting and building my resume, getting suited up, and traveling to job fairs all across the country with the hope of using those job fairs to secure a place to work.

Rather than putting God at the forefront of the interviews I had, I put more faith in my own ability to conquer what needed to be done. I idolized the path of life that having a master's degree enabled me to have, and I valued those ways higher than the ways God had intended for my life.

> For I am not ashamed of the gospel, because it is the power of God
> that brings salvation to everyone who believes: first to the Jew, then to
> the Gentile. For in the gospel the righteousness of God is revealed—a
> righteousness that is by faith from first to last, just as it is written: "The
> righteous will live by faith." Romans 1:16–17 NIV

We display our faith by our actions and by placing trust in something. Our world's ways are far from morally right, but God's ways always have proper morals.

By placing our faith in God's ways, we also place trust in his morals. Trusting God may seem like a risky thing to do in a world that runs so much differently than God does. However, if we place our faith in God, we will find righteousness, and our world will see justice in ways it has never seen before.

How are you living by faith?

_____

_____

_____

_____

How have you seen God's power at work as a result of faith?

_____

_____

_____

_____

Lesson 4: Merit

The world we live in has no problem telling us what we deserve. More often than not, those messages come in the context of what we *don't* deserve. People and groups all over the world are speaking out on the unfair treatment they receive. All of the racism, sexism, and other discriminations present on earth come from treating others in a way they don't deserve. Any time discrimination is present, it results in a lack of justice.

In the definition of *just* that signifies "being what is merited," we see that justice comes as a product of something—but what exactly is that?

Merit: *verb* to be worthy of or entitled or liable to; earn, deserve[27]

---

27 *Merriam-Webster's Dictionary and Thesaurus,* Updated Edition, s.v. "Merit."

Justice in this nature comes when people receive what they deserve. If a man and a woman have the same resume, then they are both worthy of receiving the same pay. If people of two different races earn the same transcript in school, then they both are worthy of receiving the same opportunities to go to college. Seems pretty simple when put that way, right? Our world seems to think otherwise, or at least acts like it's not that simple. Unlike God, our world isn't just—people often receive treatment they don't deserve.

A couple of months before I finished graduate school, I found myself in one of these places. My landlords came to me with the news that they were moving and presented me with a thirty-day notice to relocate. While they did so gracefully and with good intentions, I hadn't done anything personally that required me to relocate, and I immediately found myself in a bind. School was ending soon, and I didn't yet have a full-time job lined up. I didn't know if I would find a job in Utah, so I didn't want to commit to another permanent residency yet. The uncertainty related to my housing situation created a lot of fear and worry, but I had no choice—I had to act anyway and find a solution. I just wasn't sure what that solution looked like.

When was a time you were treated in a way you didn't deserve? How did the lack of justice make you feel?

_____

_____

_____

_____

We all know the pain that comes from being treated in a way we don't deserve in one way or another, and God is not numb to those feelings. Just as we treat other human beings in ways they don't deserve, we give God treatment he doesn't deserve. What kind of treatment does God deserve?

> Great is the LORD and most worthy of praise; his greatness no one can fathom. Psalm 145:3 NIV

"I call upon the LORD, who is worthy to be praised, and I am saved from my enemies." 2 Samuel 22:4 ESV

For great is the LORD and most worthy of praise; he is to be feared above all gods. 1 Chronicles 16:25 NIV

Above all else, God is worthy of our *praise*. Why?

Praise: *verb* to express approval of[28]

Everything God does is for our good. God saves us from our enemies, and his vast goodness exceeds our comprehension. If that isn't something worthy of expressing warm approval or admiration toward, then I'm not sure what or who is worthy of our praise.

What was the last thing you praised God for and why?

_____

_____

_____

_____

How do you show God praise?

_____

_____

_____

_____

It's one thing to say that God is worthy of our praise, and it's another to actually show praise. There isn't one "right" way to show praise, but a few different ways we can show praise to God are:

Songs: *The LORD protects and defends me; I trust in him. He gives me help and makes me glad; I praise him with joyful songs. Psalm 28:7*

---

28 *Merriam-Webster's Dictionary and Thesaurus,* Updated Edition, s.v. "Praise."

Accepting others: *Accept one another, then, just as Christ accepted you, in order to bring praise to God. Romans 15:7 NIV*

Proclaiming his name: *Give praise to the LORD, proclaim his name; make known among the nations what he has done. Psalm 105:1 NIV*

In the middle of this season when I was trying to figure out where to live and work, God guided me to a place of making praise to him more of a priority in my life. While I did sing praise to him at church and accept those around me, I didn't intentionally make sure that my days included an element of praising God. As I tried to figure out the next steps for my life, some friends from church presented me with an opportunity for a room I could stay in to finish the last couple of months of the school year.

Shortly after moving into that room, the trials in my life continued to pour down. On three separate occasions in a single week, my purse and all that was in it was stolen, my car was totaled, and my laptop was stepped on and destroyed. I quickly found myself in a place with no license or credit cards, no transportation, and no computer with which to finish my schoolwork. Saying I felt defeated was an understatement—what on earth did I do to deserve all of this?

Sitting in my room with nowhere to go, I was invited to a friend's house for dinner; my friend offered to give me a ride since I had no car. Upon dropping me off back home, they gave me a bag of food to hold me over until I could get a new debit card and license. In the bag was a card. While in bed later that night, I opened the card, and enough money fell onto my chest to cover not only a new license and buying a new purse, but also to make repairs to my laptop and pay my insurance deductible.

Instantly in tears, I was speechless. God made sure that despite everything I went through that week, everything was still okay. Praising his name in that moment was all I could do. He protected me and defended me just as those verses declare, and praise was the only *just* response to give back to him.

God protects us, defends us, helps us, and accepts us, and he is more than worthy and deserving of our praise. The least we can do for God in return for all he has done for us is to bring him praise by singing joyful songs, accepting those around us, and proclaiming his name.

Between joyful songs, accepting others, and proclaiming God's name, which do you find the most difficult way to bring praise to God and why?

_____

_____

_____

_____

How has God protected, defended, helped, or accepted you? Did you praise him for what he did? Why or why not?

_____

_____

_____

_____

~⌐

Dear God,

You are a God who is perfectly just, and you do nothing without reason. I know the wages of my sin is death, but because of your justice-filled nature, you chose to pay the wage of that death for me. Give me your strength to overcome the desire to conform to the standards of this world, because our world's standards do not produce the kind of justice you desire. I want to be transformed by you and have a renewed mind, because being controlled by my human nature results in death, while being controlled by your Spirit brings life and peace. It is in you alone that I can be considered righteous because you were victorious over death, and you offer to share that victory with me. You are a God that is worthy of praise. Thank you for your willingness to protect, defend, help, and accept me and for being a perfect example of justice in all circumstances.

In Jesus' name,
Amen.

Chapter Six

GOD IS TRUE

Lesson 1: Allegiance

Of all the characteristics of God's nature, the fact that he is a God who is *true* ranks among my favorites, and that's because God's truth offers freedom.

To the Jews who had believed him, Jesus said, "If you hold to my teaching, you are really my disciples. Then you will know the truth, and the truth will set you free." John 8:31–32 NIV

God's truth holds the key to setting us free, but how do we achieve that freedom? Those verses state two key ingredients to obtaining this freedom—when we *believe* in Jesus we are set free from the bondage of our sin, and when we *hold on* to the teaching with which Jesus provided us it frees us from the attacks of the enemy. Those two things can be a lot easier said than done when living in a world that is against God. Both believing in Jesus and holding onto his teachings are responses that require us to *take action*, and we can't take either of those actions unless we first make the decision internally that it's in our best interest to do so.

By exploring what God's truth looks like on a deeper level, I pray it brings us all to that place of making the decision that it's worth it to believe in Jesus and follow his teachings. How does God embody this attribute of truth? For starters, God is true with his word.

All your words are true; all your righteous laws are eternal. Psalm 119:160 NIV

Truth is the essence of God's word, and God never contradicts his word. This makes God someone in whom we can place our faith, knowing that we will be taken care of. God is good, he loves us unconditionally, and he would never call us to take a step of faith only to let us down.

While all of these things about God's nature of truth are great, being true goes so much deeper than being the opposite of the words *false* or *bad*. What else can we learn about God by knowing his nature of truth?

> **True:** *adjective* faithful in allegiance; free from fraud or deception; consistent[29]

One aspect of holding true to something requires us to show *allegiance*. We in the United States are taught allegiance at an early age; many of us grew up reciting the Pledge of Allegiance at the beginning of school each day.

> **Allegiance:** *noun* loyalty to a person or cause[30]

Regardless of the nature of the person or cause to which we show loyalty, every one of us shows allegiance to something or someone. How do we choose what we will show our allegiance to? In the selfishness of our human nature, we choose to show allegiance and loyalty to people or causes that give us benefit.

What is a person or cause you have shown loyalty to and why?

_____

_____

_____

_____

While the list of people and things we can show our allegiance to is endless, God wants us to place our allegiance in *him*. Is placing allegiance in God for our benefit? A large problem our world has with placing allegiance in God is that our world is often blind to the benefit God offers us.

---

29 *Merriam-Webster's Dictionary and Thesaurus,* Updated Edition, s.v. "True."
30 *Merriam-Webster's Dictionary and Thesaurus,* Updated Edition, s.v. "Allegiance."

Soon after God miraculously provided for me financially to cover all the trials life threw at me, he presented me with an opportunity to show my allegiance to him. The week I graduated with my MBA, I received a job offer to become a data analyst—a job that enabled me to stay in Utah. Finally having a stable schedule for the first time in my entire adult life, I pondered how I could get more involved in church.

Falling back on my passion for women's ministry, I spoke with a couple of other women about doing something I had desired to do for years—lead my own small group. They encouraged me to figure out exactly what this group would look like. Not even ten minutes after they presented me with that question, God made the answer clear to me. He said, "If you want to lead that group, Emily, you need to start *writing*."

In that moment, I needed to decide whether God was worth showing allegiance to. Why? Because being a writer was the *last* thing I wanted to do. I really wanted to pursue leading this group, whatever it looked like, but couldn't I get there some other way, God? My initial answer to the question of whether it was worth it to show God this level of allegiance was *no*. And that answer came mainly out of fear.

While fear kept me from initially saying yes, that call to start writing continued to roam in the back of my mind. Should I respond to this call and be loyal to God? I didn't know how to respond, but thankfully, God sets the example for us in what it looks like to show allegiance. Of course, God didn't also grow up in school pledging his allegiance each morning, but he does show his allegiance in other ways. God shows his loyalty and is true to:

> **Himself:** *"If we are not faithful, he remains faithful, because he cannot be false to himself." 2 Timothy 2:13*
>
> **Us:** *LORD, I know you will never stop being merciful to me. Your love and loyalty will always keep me safe. Psalm 40:11*

What do you think Paul means when he mentions that God cannot be false to himself?

Has God's love and loyalty to you ever allowed you to feel safe? If so, how?

_____

_____

_____

_____

First and foremost, God stays true to *himself.* Why is this important? It means that God is who he says he is, and he always does what he says he's going to do. We can *always* count on God, and that will *never* change.

God also remains loyal and true to *us.* Even when we don't show our faithfulness to God, he remains faithful to us and loves us—who else can say that? No one, that's who. God's loyalty to us keeps us *safe.* Does that mean life will be easy? No. What it does mean is that God will never leave us in the dust. His mercy and love never end, and he won't ever be any other way because he stays true to himself always.

How has God stayed faithful to you even when you weren't faithful to him?

_____

_____

_____

_____

What is an area of life in which you could show more loyalty to God, and what is a step you will take toward doing so?

_____

_____

_____

_____

Lesson 2: Fraud

Advancements in technology and all of the capabilities electronics provide us with give us extreme levels of convenience. Almost any task in our everyday life can be done from an application on our phone, and social media enables us to connect with people all over the world in a matter of seconds. There's no question that these capabilities provide us with benefits. However, they also come with some setbacks, one of which is the ease of committing fraud.

Acts of fraud occur so often in our world that we've likely all been affected by one. Fraudulent accounts get created on social media everyday with people making fake profiles and disguising themselves as someone else. We also see fraud in our email inboxes. Spam emails flood each of our inboxes from people who try to get us to click on a special link and fill out our information, only so they can then steal our information.

People who commit fraud do so for their own gain. Any time fraud occurs, it does not come from God. How can we know that? One definition of *true* is "free from fraud." God *never* does anything for his own gain, and he has *zero* tolerance for fraud, as stated in this verse:

> *"Honor the LORD and act carefully, because the LORD our God does not tolerate fraud or partiality or the taking of bribes." 2 Chronicles 19:7*

If God doesn't tolerate fraud, and the definition of true is "free from fraud," we can conclude that God has no tolerance for anything outside of the truth. But what about all of the fraud that happens in our world? If God doesn't tolerate fraud, why does he allow it to happen?

Tolerate: *verb* to allow the existence, presence, practice, or act of without prohibition or hindrance; permit.[31]

Just because God allows acts of fraud to happen on this earth does not mean that he tolerates those acts of fraud. God allows the existence of fraud, but he *does not* allow it without prohibition or hindrance. Fraud is a *sin*, and God justly punishes all sin.

---

31 *Dictionary.com*, s.v. "Tolerate," accessed December 04, 2022, https://www.dictionary.com/

Why do you think the Bible goes so far as to say that God has no tolerance for fraud?

_____

_____

_____

_____

Unlike God, our world *does* have a tolerance for fraud—acts of fraud go on without prohibition or hindrance all the time. What is the result of this tolerance for fraud? It creates and normalizes a culture in our world where people obtain personal gain at the expense of others.

How would our world look different if it shared the same no-tolerance policy for fraud that God has?

_____

_____

_____

_____

Jesus shares in God's nature of not tolerating fraud, and he displayed that quality in his own ministry:

> *Then Jesus was led by the Spirit into the wilderness to be tempted by the devil. After fasting forty days and forty nights, he was hungry. The tempter came to him and said, "If you are the Son of God, tell these stones to become bread." Jesus answered, "It is written: 'Man shall not live on bread alone, but on every word that comes from the mouth of God.'" Then the devil took him to the holy city and had him stand on the highest point of the temple. "If you are the Son of God," he said, "throw yourself down. For it is written: "'He will command his angels concerning you, and they will lift you up in their hands, so that you will not strike your foot against a stone.'" Jesus answered him, "It is*

also written: 'Do not put the Lord your God to the test.'" Again, the devil took him to a very high mountain and showed him all the kingdoms of the world and their splendor. "All this I will give you," he said, "if you will bow down and worship me." Jesus said to him, "Away from me, Satan! For it is written: 'Worship the Lord your God, and serve him only.'" Then the devil left him, and angels came and attended him. Matthew 4:1–11 NIV

In this passage, Satan attempts to make a fraud out of Jesus. Satan knows Jesus is hungry, so he tempts Jesus by saying, *"If you are the Son of God, tell these stones to become bread." Matthew 4:3 NIV*. What is Satan trying to accomplish by saying this? I don't think Satan actually doubts that Jesus is the Son of God, but I do absolutely think that Satan wants *us* to doubt that Jesus is the Son of God!

Just as much as Satan wants us to doubt who Jesus is, he wants us to doubt *ourselves*. Have you ever felt like a fraud? Me too, all the time—especially when it comes to my walk with God. Coincidence? I don't think so. Satan hates seeing us prosper in our walks with God!

This same concept of feeling like a fraud left me feeling apprehensive about answering God's call to write. Nothing in my previous twenty-five years of life led me to believe that writing and books were involved in my life's purpose, which made for some very low-hanging fruit for Satan to attack. Similar to how Satan essentially asked Jesus to "prove himself" by turning the stones to bread, he said to me, "You? A writer? Prove it." I didn't have the confidence in myself to prove it, so instead I did nothing, which is *exactly* what Satan wanted me to do. Talk about an effective attack mechanism!

What is the difference between Satan and God in all of this? God never asked me to prove *anything*; he simply wanted me to trust in his plan. Satan *knows* God holds more power than he does, and he hates that. He hates it so much, that he tries to twist God's words in any way he can in an attempt to make God look like a fraud. Jesus responds to these attempts by quoting the words of the one true God, saying, *"It is written: 'Man shall not live on bread alone, but on every word that comes from the mouth of God.'" Matthew 4:4 NIV*

What do you think it means to live on every word that comes from the mouth of God?

_____

_____

_____

_____

Satan follows up his temptation by trying to bribe Jesus. He tells Jesus that he will give him a kingdom if Jesus bows down to worship him. Jesus has no tolerance for this bribe and immediately follows Satan's bribe by telling him to go away. Jesus spoke truth to Satan by saying we are to serve and worship God alone. With that, Satan left Jesus.

Just as God has no tolerance for fraud, Satan has no tolerance for the truth. We may not have the power to eradicate Satan's presence from this earth, but we do have the power to choose who we worship. When we worship God, Satan and his fraud do not have power over us.

Why do you think Satan tried to convince Jesus to worship him?

_____

_____

_____

_____

What is one way you can further place your worship in God alone?

_____

_____

_____

_____

Lesson 3: Deception

Have you ever thought someone was lying when they told you their age? I know I have; looks can be *deceiving*. Our world places a high value on looking "young." The older we get, the more the world tries to convince us to buy this new product or to get that surgery in order to deceive others into thinking we're younger than our actual age. Anytime deception occurs, the one doing the deceiving tries to get someone to believe something other than the truth. That's why we see *true* defined as "free from deception."[32]

When was a time you were deceived? How were you deceived, and what was the truth behind that deception?

_____

_____

_____

_____

Although the Word of God is in itself truth and free from deception, it does speak of deception. We live in a world full of deception, and we need more awareness of what deception looks like and how to find freedom from it.

The enemy wastes no time in his attempts to deceive us. After Adam and Eve sinned and ate of the forbidden fruit, the following conversation took place:

> *Then the LORD God said to the woman, "What is this you have done?"*
> *The woman said, "The serpent deceived me, and I ate." Genesis 3:13 NIV*

Why do you think Eve specifically tells God that she ate the fruit because of deception?

_____

_____

_____

_____

---

32 *Merriam-Webster's Dictionary and Thesaurus*, Updated Edition, s.v. "True."

A few verses earlier in Genesis, we see the deception to which Eve refers:

Now the snake was the most cunning animal that the LORD God had made. The snake asked the woman, "Did God really tell you not to eat fruit from any tree in the garden?" "We may eat the fruit of any tree in the garden," the woman answered, "except the tree in the middle of it. God told us not to eat the fruit of that tree or even touch it; if we do, we will die." The snake replied, "That's not true; you will not die. God said that because he knows that when you eat it, you will be like God and know what is good and what is bad." Genesis 3:1–5

It's important to acknowledge the intelligence of the serpent. The serpent knew *exactly* what the truth was and purposefully spoke to Eve in a way to get her to question the truth. He deceives Eve by coming across as harmless and then blatantly lies to her by saying how it isn't true that she will die if she eats the fruit.

This scenario is as true for us today as it was for Eve. Anything wanting to convince us to question the truth of God's Word comes from a source of *deception*. God is true, free of deception, and wants us to find freedom from the deception in this world.

Do not be deceived: God cannot be mocked. A man reaps what he sows. Whoever sows to please their flesh, from the flesh will reap destruction; whoever sows to please the Spirit, from the Spirit will reap eternal life. Galatians 6:7–8 NIV

God didn't deceive Adam and Eve, and he won't deceive us, either. He warned Adam and Eve not to eat the fruit and told them exactly what would happen if they did. Likewise, we are warned in this Galatians passage to not be deceived and give in to the flesh or we will reap destruction.

When have you done something to please the flesh and what destruction came as a result?

_____

_____

_____

_____

We do not have to allow our flesh to control us, nor do we have to reap the destruction that comes from it. God is free from that deception, and he offers his Spirit generously to all who are willing to receive it. From that Spirit, we have God's power to overcome deception and are able to reap an eternal life with God that is also free from deception.

I sat down to write for the first time about two months after having that initial conversation in which God told me that I needed to start writing. Did I make this move because I magically changed my view of myself? Definitely not. I chose to figure out what this "writing" thing looked like because I didn't want to allow my limited view of myself to have control over me. On my own power, my view of my writing capabilities would never change, but with God's power through the Holy Spirit, I could overcome that deception and discover the life that God had waiting for me.

That afternoon, I stepped into an adventure with God far greater than my mind could comprehend. I remained very narrow-minded about where this writing journey would go; all I ever really expected from it was to have a few women come to my house and discuss whatever topics my writing led to. While I didn't know where my life was heading, I knew God was pleased with my decision to pursue writing. Whatever result would come from this decision would be all by his grace because I was clueless.

When have you done something to please the Spirit and what was the result?

_____

_____

_____

_____

Have you ever felt free from the deception of this world? If so, how did you obtain that freedom? If not, what gets in your way of obtaining that freedom?

_____

_____

_____

_____

〜⌇

Lesson 4: Consistency

Imagine you come home from work one day, open your mail, and come across a letter summoning you to jury duty. You make it past the candidate screening and find yourself sitting in on a case. Regardless of the nature of the case, you observe the trial to help determine who did what. It's your job to give a verdict for the case based off of what you know to be *true*. One of the ways to uncover the truth is to look for consistencies—does what the witnesses say line up with the evidence presented?

This concept of being true applies for any people or products in which we invest—are their actions consistent with their word? Are they staying true to who or what they claim to be? None of us will always live up to who we claim to be. That may sound discouraging, but I don't say that to make you feel terrible about yourself—it simply means that you are human and not God.

Unlike us, God always stays true to himself, and Jesus as the Son of God displays this characteristic for us in the flesh.

Jesus Christ is the same yesterday and today and forever. Hebrews 13:8 ESV

How does the fact that the nature of Jesus never changes allow you to interact with him differently than you would someone else?

_____

_____

_____

_____

Knowing that Jesus is the same yesterday, today, and forever is important, but its importance holds more depth if we know *how* he's the same. Who is Jesus, and to what does he hold true? There are hundreds of characteristics of Jesus, but for now we'll stick to just a few of them:

> **Patient:** *Here is a trustworthy saying that deserves full acceptance: Christ Jesus came into the world to save sinners—of whom I am the worst. But for that very reason I was shown mercy so that in me, the worst of sinners, Christ Jesus might display his immense patience as an example for those who would believe in him and receive eternal life. 1 Timothy 1:15–16 NIV*
>
> **Forgiving:** *Be kind and compassionate to one another, forgiving each other, just as in Christ God forgave you. Ephesians 4:32 NIV*
>
> **Light:** *When Jesus spoke again to the people, he said, "I am the light of the world. Whoever follows me will never walk in darkness, but will have the light of life." John 8:12 NIV*

How has the patience, forgiveness, or light of Jesus been displayed in your own life?

_____

_____

_____

_____

How could you use more of God's patience, forgiveness, or light right now?

_____

_____

_____

_____

Not only does Jesus remain true and consistent in his actions, but he also remains true in his mission. Jesus makes his heart for us to receive life very clear in these verses. His immense patience serves as an example for us to believe in him and receive life; it also enables us to receive that life because his death has forgiven the price we owe for our sins. When we receive that payment and forgiveness for our sins, we receive God's Spirit and possess the light of life.

Jesus came to earth with a very specific mission. God has a mission, or purpose, for every one of us as well. For me, part of that mission involved writing. The million-dollar question I needed to figure out before I could begin writing was what on earth I was supposed to write about. I wanted to figure out what I should write about, but first I had to first figure out my mission and what I wanted people to get from my writing.

When I boiled it down to what I really want people to know the most, it is the *truth* spoken of in John 8:32 that sets people free. A few not-so-little-known facts about me: I'm blunt, I'm a bad liar, and I do not tolerate well people lying and deceiving me or anyone else. If someone came up to me and told me I was ugly or stupid, I would have no problem telling them to keep their negativity to themselves. I wish more people—especially women—knew the truth about their value so deeply that they were comfortable in doing the same, rather than internalizing it. From these desires, I decided what to write about. I started researching truths about how God sees us, and the beginning of what is now *Broken Lenses: Identifying Your Truth in a World of Lies* was born.

How would I accomplish this mission? Simple—*only* by leaning on the firm foundation of Jesus, who is the same yesterday, today, and forever. The patience, forgiveness, and light of Christ will always be available to us. God never wanted us to die, and that desire remains true as proven by him offering us the death of Jesus, which is the one and only way to receive eternal life. We aren't "late" if we choose to believe in Jesus at a later stage in life than someone else. We can't "mess up" our lives so much that he will refuse to forgive our sins when we turn to him. He won't leave us in the dark by offering his light only to certain people. God treats us all consistently, he stays true to his character at all times, and he sent Jesus to be a physical representation of that consistency.

Starting on this writing journey forced me out of my comfort zone in many areas and also forced me to spend *consistent* time with God and God alone. I had gone back to church and attended Bible studies for years, but those were both group settings. Being a highly extroverted person who loves group settings, those environments were comfortable, and I thrive in them.

While those things in my life were both good things, God desired a more intimate relationship with me. As uncomfortable as it was, I had to decide whether my comfort was more valuable than pursuing the life God had for me. My answer to that question was *no*. Once I decided that, in a matter of just a few days the course of my relationship with God changed forever. I just didn't know what that change would bring to my life . . . yet.

Have you ever told yourself you don't deserve the same treatment as others? If so, why?

_____

_____

_____

_____

Are you spending consistent time with God? Why or why not?

_____

_____

_____

_____

Dear God,

Thank you for being a God who is always true to himself. You are a God of truth and someone I can always count on. You have zero tolerance for fraud, and anything on this earth trying to convince me you aren't true or that you aren't for me does not come from you. I confess that at times, I allow my flesh to control me, and destruction results from that control. You are free from deception, and by your Spirit I can overcome the control of my flesh and find eternal life in you. You are the same yesterday, today, and forever, and your consistent nature allows me to have a firm foundation upon which to build my life. Teach me how to be a light to those you have placed in my life by extending patience and forgiveness, so that they may come to understand your truth as well.

In Jesus' name,
Amen.

Chapter Seven

GOD IS LIGHT

Lesson 1: Vision

The light bulb was invented well more than one hundred years ago, but to this day it is still considered one of the world's greatest inventions. Since its invention in the late 1800s, the light bulb has greatly evolved, and our society now depends on the light manufactured from them. We can't drive our cars at night without our headlights—and as soon as we walk inside the house after that night drive, what's the first thing we do? We turn on another light.

From an earthly sense, every single one of us knows the value and importance of light. I'm even willing to bet that none of you wants to live a life without light—myself included. What does light, or the importance of light, have to do with God? Light was one of the first things God created when he created this world, and the Bible describes God as being light.

This is the message we have heard from him and declare to you: God is light; in him there is no darkness at all. 1 John 1:5 NIV

The kind of light spoken of here isn't the same kind of light given off from a light bulb, but the value that God's light brings is just as valuable and important as that of the light bulb, if not more. What importance does God's light have?

Light: *noun* something that makes vision possible; a source of light (as a candle); a noteworthy person in a particular place[33]

The first aspect in understanding the importance of light is knowing that light makes vision possible. It's important to note here that the light as described in this context isn't the one that's doing the *seeing*, but rather the thing that is doing the *revealing*. The revealing that comes as a product of turning on our car's headlights or flipping the light switch in the kitchen is light we all want, or we wouldn't have turned on the light to begin with. When we get something we want, it's easy for us to value it or gravitate toward it, which explains our ever-increasing dependence on light bulbs.

Unlike manufactured light, God's light shines into the darkness of our lives. God's light makes vision possible to parts of our lives we may have never dealt with before. Often that doesn't cause a lot of excitement because we may not see the same level of value in that. None of us is perfect, and we all have things in our lives that we aren't proud of. A lot of us have things that we purposefully try to forget about, and sometimes our minds even block memories as a response to traumatic events.

Has God ever revealed or made it possible for you to see something new about yourself? If so, what?

_____

_____

_____

_____

Just because we don't always see the value in something doesn't mean that there isn't value to it. When we invite God's light into our lives, it *transforms* us. If God is light and in him there is no darkness, that means that any area of darkness in our lives that we invite God into *cannot stay dark*. Although this may sound scary or intimidating, in reality it is solely for our good. God knows what's best for us, and by living in his light we defeat the darkness that once had power over us.

---

33 *Merriam-Webster's Dictionary and Thesaurus,* Updated Edition, s.v. "Light."

You yourselves used to be in the darkness, but since you have become
the Lord's people, you are in the light. So you must live like people who
belong to the light, for it is the light that brings a rich harvest of every
kind of goodness, righteousness, and truth. Ephesians 5:8–9

I had a lot of darkness in my life when it came to writing. I even had an English professor in college once say to me that I "didn't know how to grammatically put a sentence together." Starting this new journey with God and entering an area of darkness in my life was intimidating. At the same time, staying in my darkness would only strip me of all of the goodness, righteousness, and truth that God wanted to bring to my life through this journey.

What do you think it looks like to live like people who belong to the light?

_____

_____

_____

_____

Where could you use more goodness, righteousness, or truth in your life right now?

_____

_____

_____

_____

That passage in Ephesians exclaims that we should live like people who belong to the light, but how is that done?

"You are the light of the world. A town built on a hill cannot be hidden.
Neither do people light a lamp and put it under a bowl. Instead they
put it on its stand, and it gives light to everyone in the house. In the
same way, let your light shine before others, that they may see your good
deeds and glorify your Father in heaven." Matthew 5:14–16 NIV

If we live like people who belong to the light, that means we cannot hide. That's not all—we're not even supposed to *pretend* like we can hide. As far as my writing was concerned, I did a great job of attempting to hide my light. When I first committed to writing, I was very adamant about not including my life story in the content. In doing this, I failed to allow God to shine through me and to use my story for his glory. It also kept me in my comfort zone. I didn't want God to shine his light the into dark areas of my life because I didn't want to confront my darkness in order to write about it.

Being a child of God, and therefore a person who belongs to the light, brings glory to God. Light is intended to be seen—it makes vision possible—and we have no need or reason to allow the darkness of this world to stop us from shining God's light to others. Anything that causes fear and prevents us from inviting God into the dark spaces of our lives and being a light to the world *does not* come from God. God is the source of the light that we are called to shine to the world, and the *last* thing he wants to do is put out that light in us and keep us in darkness!

How do you shine your light before others?

_____

_____

_____

_____

Are you allowing the darkness of this world to prevent you from shining God's light? If so, how?

_____

_____

_____

_____

Lesson 2: Source

In the world of science, light is described as a form of energy. Although light physically comes in many different colors and wavelengths, all light is energy. As described in the first law of thermodynamics, one truth about all forms of energy is that energy cannot be created or destroyed. The energy used to produce any form of light has a *source* where it came from or how it was produced.

The definition of light points to this concept, stating, "a source of light (as a candle)."[34] This definition may sound confusing, given the fact that the word being defined is also included in the definition, but what is this definition getting at? Before electricity readily existed in homes, people used candles as a primary source of light. Although the fire from the candle produces a physical light, the fire can't exist or be sustained unless it has a source from which it can burn.

In the previous lesson, we saw in the book of Matthew that Jesus called us to be a light to the world. This isn't possible on our own power, so how do we fulfill this calling? We *can* be a light to the world, but we *can't* be that light to the world without having a source for that light, and that's where God comes in.

> *In the beginning was the Word, and the Word was with God, and the Word was God. He was with God in the beginning. Through him all things were made; without him nothing was made that has been made. In him was life, and that life was the light of all mankind.*
> *John 1:1–4 NIV*

Do you look to God to be the source of your light? Why or why not?

_____

_____

_____

_____

There is a light that acts as a source of light for each and every one of us, and that light comes in the form of a life. That passage points to Jesus as being

---

34 *Merriam-Webster's Dictionary and Thesaurus,* Updated Edition, s.v. "Light."

that one life is the source of light for all mankind. We are called to spread that light to the world, and continuing on in the book of John, we see John doing just that.

> There was a man sent from God whose name was John. He came as a witness to testify concerning that light, so that through him all might believe. He himself was not the light; he came only as a witness to the light. John 1:6–8 NIV

Witness: *noun* one who has personal knowledge of something[35]

What does being a witness to the light mean to you?

_____

_____

_____

_____

Has anyone ever witnessed to you about the light? If so, what impact did that witness have on you?

_____

_____

_____

_____

John states that he witnesses to the light so that all might believe. If John committed his life so that all might believe, there has to be a good reason for it, right? What does John hope that others will believe, and why is he willing to commit so much of his life to it?

> The true light that gives light to everyone was coming into the world. He was in the world, and though the world was made through him, the world did not recognize him. He came to that which was his own,

---

35 *Merriam-Webster.com,* s.v. "Witness," accessed December 04, 2022, https://www.merriam-webster.com/

but his own did not receive him. Yet to all who did receive him, to
those who believed in his name, he gave the right to become children of
God—children born not of natural descent, nor of human decision or
a husband's will, but born of God. John 1:9–13 NIV

We see here that the Word that gives light to all mankind is Jesus, and Jesus is the light of which we are called to be witnesses. All too often, our world underestimates the power of being a witness—either that or they're just unclear what our call is as Christians. For those of you who call yourselves believers of Jesus, how have you seen any benefit in your life as a result of that belief? If you're able to answer that question having clearly seen the benefit that a life in Jesus offers, how can you *not* want to share that goodness and witness to the people around you?

Jesus came into this world and shined a light to all who crossed his path. The world did not recognize Jesus, though, which is where we come into play. God will never *force* us to witness of his light. Being a witness for the sake of Christ needs to come from the willingness of our own hearts. Being unashamed of our beliefs is a lot easier said than done in a world where bearing that witness often comes with a stigma.

Writing sent me down a path of witnessing to a greater degree than ever before, and honestly, it was uncomfortable. Luckily, I had the safety blanket of my day job as a data analyst. For the entirety of the time that it took me to write my first book, I lived this double life of pursuing the corporate life by day, going to a coffee shop to write until midnight, and then waking up the next day to do it all over again.

Whenever someone asked me how my writing was going, it provided an open door to bear witness to God's light. Open doors are great, but open doors do no good unless we walk through them. God uses people like us and like John to bring the light of Jesus into this world so that others might believe. When we place our belief in Jesus, we become children of God. As children of God, we receive something that the world will never be able to give us—the light of life. The light of life that Jesus offers us is unlike anything this world has to offer. When we bear witness to that light and its undeniable goodness, the world has no choice but to take notice.

Why do you think the world did not recognize Jesus?

_____

_____

_____

_____

What is something that is preventing you from being a witness to someone in your life right now, and how can you ask God to shine his light into that situation?

_____

_____

_____

_____

Lesson 3: Noteworthy

Have you ever gotten so caught up in day-to-day living that you couldn't remember what day it was? Day-to-day living looks different for each of us, but we all have things to which we devote a consistent amount of time. When all of our days look relatively the same, they become easily forgettable. Every once in a while, we encounter a person who breaks up that monotony. We meet them, and we may not know why or how, but they *light up* the room. These people fall under the type of light defined as "a noteworthy person in a particular place."

Who is a noteworthy person you have met? Where were you, and what about them gave off light?

_____

_____

_____

_____

Noteworthy people we meet often leave an impression on us. They have the power to alter the mood of our days, or even our lives. The lasting power of being this kind of light to others impacts the entire world for good. Jesus spent his whole life being this kind of light. His life here on earth was nothing short of noteworthy.

Noteworthy: *adjective* worthy of notice or attention; notable; remarkable[36]

From the time that Jesus was born of a virgin until the time he died and rose from the grave, Jesus lived a remarkable life worthy of notice and attention. Many people had their doubts about Jesus being the person he claimed to be, but regardless of their doubt, Jesus lived a life that people couldn't help but notice.

> *Jesus left there and went to his hometown, accompanied by his disciples. When the Sabbath came, he began to teach in the synagogue, and many who heard him were amazed. "Where did this man get these things?" they asked. "What's this wisdom that has been given him? What are these remarkable miracles he is performing? Isn't this the carpenter? Isn't this Mary's son and the brother of James, Joseph, Judas and Simon? Aren't his sisters here with us?" And they took offense at him. Mark 6:1–3 NIV*

Has Jesus done anything remarkable or noteworthy in your life? If so, what?

_____

_____

_____

_____

In this passage, we see Jesus being a light while teaching in the synagogue. The people witnessing Jesus couldn't help but be amazed, and they even call out the fact that Jesus performs remarkable miracles. All of this sounds great to start, but the people who call out these remarkable miracles also make Jesus sound anything but great. The very next sentence following their acknowledgment of Jesus's wisdom and miracle-working ways consists of doubt and questioning of Jesus's validity. *"Isn't this the carpenter?"* they ask.

---

36   *Dictionary.com,* s.v. "Noteworthy," accessed December 04, 2022, https://www.dictionary.com/

They question Jesus's occupation, they question his family, and to top it all off, after all of their questioning, they take offense at Jesus. The people questioning Jesus were no different than people in our world today. Should we step out into the world and be a light ourselves, our world quickly brings judgment against us. We step out to do something notable, and all of a sudden, we hear things like, "Are you sure you want to do that?" and "Are you qualified to do that?"

I would be lying if I said I haven't heard similar remarks from the people in my life as I have walked down this writing journey. Those remarks often come from the people I expected to support me the *most*. I know I am far from alone in having this experience. I also know how painful it can be when all you want is for those people to embrace and support you in your new adventure. Why, then, do we so often experience the opposite?

If you ask me, the answer to that question lies in how those people respond to Jesus—they think they know who we are. In the minds of those in the synagogue, Jesus wasn't full of wisdom or a miracle-worker; he was a *carpenter*. Similarly, in the minds of people who had been in my life for many years, I wasn't an author; I was a chemist and a mathematician. Clearly, those things can't go together, right? Of course, that isn't true, but it's really hard to not believe that lie when multiple people throw that same doubt onto your path.

Have you ever felt opposition from the world when trying to do something notable? If so, when, and what did the world say to you?

_____

_____

_____

_____

So, what do we do when the world throws doubt our way? Jesus heard the doubt and offense of those around him, but he *did not* allow their words to affect the fact that he came to earth to be a light.

> Jesus said to them, "A prophet is not without honor except in his own town, among his relatives and in his own home." He could not do any

miracles there, except lay his hands on a few sick people and heal them.
He was amazed at their lack of faith. Mark 6:4–6 NIV

In his response to the people's offense, Jesus did a couple of noteworthy things. First, he did not let their offense affect his view of who he was—a man who worked miracles. Second, Jesus was on a mission. He came to do all for which God sent him to earth, and no one's negativity prevented that from happening. He acknowledged the people's lack of faith, but he did not allow their lack of faith to extinguish his light.

While I realize it's not easy, we don't have to allow people's lack of faith in us extinguish our light, either. As much as the people in our lives may love us, they *don't* always know what is best for us. The *only* one who always knows what is best for us is God. If God calls us to something, we don't need to wait for the approval of our world to move forward with that calling!

In this sense, we all have a lesson to learn from Jesus. God uses us to be his light to the world, just as Jesus was a light to the world in his time on earth. The world can say what it wants, but what it can't do is extinguish God's light.

Do you see yourself as a person who is noteworthy, or worthy of notice or attention? Why or why not?

_____

_____

_____

_____

Do you think God sees you as a person who is noteworthy, or worthy of notice or attention? Why or why not?

_____

_____

_____

_____

Lesson 4: Darkness
What is something you're afraid of and why?

_____

_____

_____

_____

The Bible repeatedly tells us "do not be afraid," but the truth is, fear captivates all of us at some point. While fear of things such as spiders, heights, and public speaking are among some of the more common fears in our world, I'm willing to bet that the fear of darkness has impacted each of us at some point in life.

In my own life, darkness was a key component of my greatest fear for most of my childhood. Darkness meant that bedtime was approaching, and with bedtime approaching, I would then be faced with the constant nightmares and the deeply rooted fear of being alone. Whether our fear is of the actual darkness itself or of an effect that the darkness causes, I know I'm not alone in being a victim to the effects of darkness. But should we allow the darkness to have that significant impact?

At the beginning of this chapter, we saw that, _"God is light; in him there is no darkness at all." 1 John 1:5 NIV_ Knowing that God is light and that there is no darkness in him means that we can gain understanding of God's character not only by knowing how to recognize the characteristics of light, but also by knowing how to recognize the characteristics of darkness. If we know and understand what darkness consists of, we can call out that darkness and cast it out by the power of God's light. What characteristics does darkness manifest?

> **Hate:** _But anyone who hates a brother or sister is in the darkness and walks around in the darkness. They do not know where they are going, because the darkness has blinded them. 1 John 2:11 NIV_
>
> **Evil:** _This is the verdict: Light has come into the world, but people loved darkness instead of light because their deeds were evil. John 3:19 NIV_
>
> **Fruitlessness:** _Have nothing to do with the fruitless deeds of darkness, but rather expose them. Ephesians 5:11 NIV_

Where have you experienced hate, evil, or fruitlessness in your life?

_____

_____

_____

_____

Has bringing any previous areas of darkness in your life to the light helped you overcome past evil, hate, or fruitlessness? If so, how?

_____

_____

_____

_____

If darkness produces hate, evil, and fruitlessness, and there is no darkness in God, then that means God plays *no part* in any hate, evil, or fruitlessness. This also means that as children of God, we can overcome each of these things by his light.

> *When Jesus spoke again to the people, he said, "I am the light of the world. Whoever follows me will never walk in darkness, but will have the light of life." John 8:12 NIV*

As the light of life for all mankind, Jesus gives us access to light and a life free from the powers of darkness. God is not the ultimate source of hate, evil, and fruitlessness, but instead is the ultimate source of:

> **Love:** *And so we know and rely on the love God has for us. God is love. Whoever lives in love lives in God, and God in them. 1 John 4:16 NIV*
>
> **Goodness:** *"Why do you call me good?" Jesus answered. "No one is good—except God alone." Mark 10:18 NIV*
>
> **Fruitfulness:** *"I am the vine; you are the branches. If you remain in me and I in you, you will bear much fruit; apart from me you can do nothing." John 15:5 NIV*

God's light is accessible to all of us as long as we're willing to receive the sacrifice Jesus made for us and our sins. God is the very definition of love, goodness, and fruitfulness. If we want to live a life based in love, goodness, and fruitfulness, we must find our life in the source of light and life, not in darkness. To find this life, we must first surrender our sinfulness and lifestyle of darkness.

While staying in darkness isn't for our good, we all still do it. One of the reasons we do that is because staying in darkness appears to keep us "safe." For some reason, after I started writing, I tried to control the impact of my writing even though writing was never my idea to begin with. Sounds silly when put that way, right? I knew God wanted good things for me, but stepping out into the light in areas of my life that were in the darkness for decades is scary.

The question is, at what point do we quit allowing fear to run our lives and start relying on God's love? I didn't start relying on God's love for me and for my writing until I was willing to get *uncomfortable*. When we try to control things in our lives, we can only control them within our realm of understanding. The problem with this mindset is that we worship a God who is beyond our understanding. Sometimes God just flat out doesn't make sense, and that's okay! Why is it okay? Because God wants nothing but *good* for us, and when we know that with full assurance, relying on his love becomes second nature.

Do you rely on the love God has for you? Why or why not?

_____

_____

_____

_____

How can you shine God's light and be an example of love, goodness, or fruitfulness to someone in your life right now?

_____

_____

_____

_____

Dear God,

You are a God of light, and in you there is no darkness. You call me to live in your light, for when I do, it brings a harvest full of goodness, righteousness, and truth. Nothing on this earth is hidden from you, and anything trying to tell me I need to hide from you is a lie. Reveal to me the ways that you call me to shine your light to those around me so that they may see your glory and goodness. Your Son's life is the light to all mankind, and you call me to be a witness to that light. Thank you for overcoming the hate and evil found in this world. Because of your love and goodness, I have no reason to be afraid of anything of this world. I come to you now and surrender the darkness in my heart, so that by your love and light I can be transformed into the person you called and created me to be.

In Jesus' name,
Amen.

Chapter Eight

GOD IS HOLY

Lesson 1: Devotion

If I asked you to explain God's holiness to me, what would you say?

_____

_____

_____

_____

The holiness of God gets mentioned in many worship songs. We sing about it, but we don't really talk about it. Why is that?

Holiness is such a big part of God's character that it's in the name of his Spirit—the Holy Spirit. Anyone who prays to receive Jesus's payment for their sins receives God's Holy Spirit, but why is that a big deal? What makes something holy, and how does God fit the definition of being holy?

> **Holy:** _adjective_ worthy of absolute devotion; to be treated with veneration or the utmost respect; sacred[37]

---

37 _Merriam-Webster's Dictionary and Thesaurus,_ Updated Edition, s.v. "Holy."

Let's first look at seeing something as "worthy of absolute devotion." There are three layers to this definition of holiness. The first of those layers is *devotion*. Whether to God or to something or someone else, each of us shows devotion. To be devoted to something requires us to show commitment. The question is, what does that commitment look like?

> **Devoted:** *adjective* zealous or ardent in attachment, loyalty, or affection; faithful; constant; loyal[38]

What is something to which you are devoted, and why do you choose to be devoted to it?

_____

_____

_____

_____

To treat something as holy—with absolute devotion—means we that we show it consistency, loyalty, and faithfulness. In order to relate to God as holy, we must show that consistency, loyalty, and faithfulness toward *him*. We make choices daily on where to show our loyalty and faithfulness, but not everything to which we devote those qualities is holy. What is the difference?

The difference lies in the second layer of that definition of *holy*. To be holy, something must be *worthy* of our devotion. How do we know that God is worthy of that treatment? God demonstrates his worthiness of our absolute devotion by first being absolutely devoted to *us* by being:

> **Faithful:** *if we are faithless, he remains faithful, for he cannot disown himself. 2 Timothy 2:13 NIV*
>
> **Loyal:** *LORD, I know you will never stop being merciful to me. Your love and loyalty will always keep me safe. Psalm 40:11*
>
> **Constant:** *How precious, O God, is your constant love! We find protection under the shadow of your wings. Psalm 36:7*

---

38 *Dictionary.com*, s.v. "Devoted," accessed December 04, 2022, https://www.dictionary.com/

Have you ever experienced the faithfulness, loyalty, or constant love that God has for you? If so, how did seeing his devotion to you make you feel?

_____

_____

_____

_____

Have you ever shown God your faithfulness, loyalty, or consistency? If so, how did he respond to your devotion to him?

_____

_____

_____

_____

God paves the way for us to know how to relate to something as holy by first showing his devotion to us. He relates to us as if we were holy, but none of us shows that same level of devotion to him in return—our sinful nature gets in our way. Our sin places a barrier for us to truly relate to God as a God who is holy. Why? Because the third layer of this definition of holiness says that we are to show *absolute* devotion.

Showing absolute devotion to God is where my own relationship with our holy God started to break down. I knew God was worth devoting time to, or I never would've started writing to begin with. However, I still held onto an identity tied to this world, so I also showed devotion to other things to fulfill that identity. I spent twenty years in school to get an education that landed me a job and a career that fit my skill set very well. I invested thousands of both hours and dollars in this career, and I wasn't willing to just "give it all up."

To no surprise, God had other ideas for my life. The longer I spent devoting my time to both writing and my career, the more I started to see the fruits of what my devotion brought in each area. As I devoted my time to writing, I began to see blessings and prosperity beyond my comprehension. I found people who devoted time out of their schedules every week to invest in me, my message, and my writing journey. I also encountered someone who had never met me before but believed in what I was doing so much that they connected me with a writing expert so that I could have a professional guide me through the process.

On the other hand, in all the time I was devoting to my job, I struggled to truly find my place of belonging. I liked what I did, and I liked my coworkers, but for some reason, I always had this sense of unfulfillment when I went home. I wanted to do more and make more of an impact, but there was always some sort of invisible roadblock in my way, and I never understood why. Hoping that things would change, I continued to devote my time in both areas.

Nothing should get in the way of us showing our devotion to God, yet we place our devotion in things of this world all the time and then act surprised when we end up feeling less than completely satisfied. We look for satisfaction from the world, when in reality we're looking for a kind of satisfaction that only God offers. Simply put, there's no one like him.

> *No one is like you, LORD; you are great, and your name is mighty in*
> *power. Jeremiah 10:6 NIV*

Why is God's demonstration of absolute devotion to us such a big deal? God wouldn't offer his constant love, loyalty, or enthusiasm for us if he didn't think we were *worth* it. In other words, God relates to *us* as being holy, and he desires the same treatment from us in return.

We can't be devoted to God and live in response to our human nature at the same time. None of us has lived a life fully devoted to God. At some point, we've all lived in response to our human nature. Luckily for us, God in his devotion to us did not withhold sacrificing his Son's life for ours. As a result of that sacrifice, God gifted us with the ability to receive his Holy Spirit. God's Holy Spirit is unlike any other spirit, and it allows us to be people who can show the same kind of love and loyalty to God that he extends to us.

What gets in your way of being devoted to God?

_____

_____

_____

_____

How can you share in God's eagerness to save and be someone who demonstrates God's love and loyalty to others?

_____

_____

_____

_____

Lesson 2: Reverence

Knowing that God is and always will be worthy of our absolute devotion is enough in itself to declare his holiness at all times. However, what if we took honoring God's holy nature a step further? How do we demonstrate our devotion to God? The next definition of *holy* suggests that we do so by showing "veneration."

If you're anything like I was while diving into research for this chapter, you're a bit unsure of what showing veneration even looks like. The word *veneration* isn't readily used in scripture, but if we look at the definition of *venerate*, we find a word that is readily used.

Venerate: *verb* to regard or treat with reverence; revere[39]

In Peter's first letter, he dedicates an entire section to addressing God's holiness and calls us to be people who show *reverence* to God.

> *Be obedient to God, and do not allow your lives to be shaped by those desires you had when you were still ignorant. Instead, be holy in all that you do, just as God who called you is holy. The scripture says, "Be holy because I am holy." You call him Father, when you pray to God, who judges all people by the same standard, according to what each one has done; so then, spend the rest of your lives here on earth in reverence for him. For you know what was paid to set you free from the worthless manner of life handed down by your ancestors. It was not something that can be destroyed, such as silver or gold; it was the*

costly sacrifice of Christ, who was like a lamb without defect or flaw.
1 Peter 1:14–19

What do you think Peter means when he writes that we are to "be holy in all that you do"?

_____

_____

_____

_____

Why is God worthy of being treated with reverence?

_____

_____

_____

_____

Peter tells us to spend the rest of our lives on earth having reverence for God. Talk about immense commitment! How are we supposed to know that making that kind of commitment is worth it? Because we are human, our nature wants to know what's in it for us in return before we make an investment—and a life-long commitment is a significant investment. Is showing reverence for God worth the devotion?

The answer to that question took me many years to figure out. The truth is, I had no clue what was in it for me in walking down my writing journey, and that made it hard to spend the rest of my life in reverence for him on that journey. So, what did I do instead? I did exactly what those verses say *not* to do: I allowed my career to continue to be shaped by the desires I had before I started writing. Allowing myself to continue to be shaped by those desires came easy, because I also wasn't doing what it says later on in the passage—remembering the costly sacrifice that Christ paid to set me free.

God knows how our human nature responds to any given situation, and the Bible graciously provides us with the answer we're looking for when it comes to why we should show reverence to God. Showing reverence to God comes with no shortage of benefits, some of which include:

> **Wisdom:** *To be wise you must first have reverence for the LORD. If you know the Holy One, you have understanding. Proverbs 9:10*
>
> **Confidence and security:** *Reverence for the LORD gives confidence and security to a man and his family. Proverbs 14:26*
>
> **Life:** *Do you want to avoid death? Reverence for the LORD is a fountain of life. Proverbs 14:27*

When you consider wisdom, confidence, security, and a fountain of life, which could you use the most of right now, and why?

_____

_____

_____

_____

Other than God, who can promise us wisdom, confidence, security, and life if we revere them or treat them as if they are holy? The answer is simple—no one. God alone is all-knowing. He is bigger than any trial we face, and when Jesus sacrificed his life on the cross for our sins, the grave could not hold him down. God can promise us wisdom, confidence, security, and life when we revere him, because those characteristics are his very nature, and nothing can ever take those away from him.

The longer I continued to devote my time to both my writing and my career, the more I felt a lack of wisdom, confidence, security, and life. After about a year of being in a role that didn't fit the department as well as they had hoped, I got transferred to a new team. I wanted more wisdom and understanding on how working in this team would fit better, but as much as I asked God for that wisdom and understanding, I still couldn't tell you to this day that I ever got the answer for which I was looking. I relied on my job significantly for confidence and security—especially financially—and to no surprise, God wasn't much of a fan of that.

To know God, the Holy One, is to have understanding. That doesn't mean we will somehow come to a place of fully understanding God—God is bigger than we can fully comprehend. But I do believe that God *wants* us to get to know him. The more we get to know God, the more we understand his goodness, how he works, and his love for us. When we truly understand those aspects of God, we can't help but revere him because we gain better understanding of his greatness.

What about God do you wish you had a better understanding of?

_____

_____

_____

_____

In what way do you think you could get to know God better in order to find that understanding?

_____

_____

_____

_____

Lesson 3: Utmost Respect

If I were to walk up to a random person and ask, "Do you desire to be treated as holy?" I don't think many of them would say they do. My guess is, though, that if we related to the word *holy* with its definition of being "treated with utmost respect,"[40] we would all change our minds and say we *do* want to be treated as holy. We all want respect, and being treated with *utmost* respect would be the icing on the cake.

---

40 *Merriam-Webster's Dictionary and Thesaurus,* Updated Edition, s.v. "Holy."

In order to relate to anything as holy, we must first know how to show respect. The kind of respect described in the definition of *holy* is a verb. That means that in order to relate to God as holy, it's not enough for us to simply *have* respect for God. Our respect for God must convict us enough to influence our *actions*. How do we show respect?

What do you respect about God, and why?

_____

_____

_____

_____

Respect: *verb* to hold in esteem or honor[41]

Respecting others comes as a product of showing esteem and honor. Sounds easy enough, right? Surely, God is worthy of us giving him honor and holding him in esteem, but do we show it to him?

> *Who has believed our message and to whom has the arm of the LORD been revealed? He grew up before him like a tender shoot, and like a root out of dry ground. He had no beauty or majesty to attract us to him, nothing in his appearance that we should desire him. He was despised and rejected by mankind, a man of suffering, and familiar with pain. Like one from whom people hide their faces he was despised, and we held him in low esteem. Surely he took up our pain and bore our suffering, yet we considered him punished by God, stricken by him, and afflicted. But he was pierced for our transgressions, he was crushed for our iniquities; the punishment that brought us peace was on him, and by his wounds we are healed. Isaiah 53:1–5 NIV*

This passage displays a prophecy of Jesus's death on the cross and gives a perfect example of God's holiness. Even when God is treated opposite to his holy nature by those who hold him in low esteem and show no respect to him, he sends

---

41 *Dictionary.com*, s.v. "Respect," accessed December 04, 2022, https://www.dictionary.com/

his Son to sacrifice his life on our behalf. Who else would do something like that? No one, that's who.

Jesus died a death we all deserve, and because of his death we get access to peace and healing. He suffered for us so we don't have to suffer, and we don't have to "prove ourselves" to earn this healing—we need only to receive the payment Jesus offers to us.

Has Jesus's suffering on your behalf healed you from any of your wounds? If so, how?

_____

_____

_____

_____

What is a wound you have that you would like to be healed, and how can you surrender that wound to God?

_____

_____

_____

_____

None of what Jesus went through was a surprise to God; all of it was part of his *will* for Jesus's life. Jesus bore the punishment none of us could take on, and for that he deserves the utmost respect, honor, and esteem.

> The LORD says, "It was my will that he should suffer; his death was a sacrifice to bring forgiveness. And so he will see his descendants; he will live a long life, and through him my purpose will succeed. After a life of suffering, he will again have joy; he will know that he did not suffer in vain. My devoted servant, with whom I am pleased, will bear the punishment of many and for his sake I will forgive them. And so I will give him a place of honor, a place among the great and

powerful. He willingly gave his life and shared the fate of evil men.
He took the place of many sinners and prayed that they might be for-
given." Isaiah 53:10–12

We don't give God the respect that his holiness deserves, but Jesus did give him that respect. Jesus devoted himself to serving God in a way none of us can do. He died to bring us forgiveness, and for his suffering, God gives Jesus a place of honor. God knows we can't honor him in the same way, but we can devote ourselves to serving him, and in doing so we will find honor.

"If anyone serves me, he must follow me; and where I am, there will
my servant be also. If anyone serves me, the Father will honor him."
John 12:26 ESV

All of us want honor, but our world looks for honor in the wrong things and places. God honors anyone who serves *him*, not *themselves*. How do we serve God? Serving God requires us to follow him over our own selfish desires.

I am just as guilty as any at looking for honor in the wrong things and places. I never expected any honor for my writing. Writing wasn't a life I ever asked for, so to be quite honest, I didn't have much desire to find honor in it. I had enormous imposter syndrome as I pursued writing, and my lack of feeling capable didn't help me feel like I deserved that kind of respect or that honor would come from my messages.

Where I *did* feel capable was in my day job, but the response I got in my time there communicated otherwise. I completed all of the training and education, and I selfishly wanted more. I knew I was capable of more than what they gave me to do. I felt like I was being kept in a box that didn't properly reflect my capabilities. One could say that I got a crash course on building relationships in the workplace during this process. When I know I'm capable of something, I don't easily allow in the opinions of people who don't agree or who try to convince me otherwise.

Unlike our selfish human nature, Jesus is not selfish, and he doesn't call us to serve him solely for *his* own gain. By serving him, *we* benefit too. No one else offers the same kind of benefits from us devoting our utmost respect, and that quality alone should be enough to want to devote all of our honor and respect to God. However, we can't serve Jesus without also following him, and we can't follow Jesus unless we drop our own agenda for our life first. God always knows what is best for our lives. We don't also have to know what that "best" is; we need only to have faith that God does and always will know best.

Do you ever have trouble following Jesus? If so, how or in what way?

_____

_____

_____

_____

What does following God look like for you right now?

_____

_____

_____

_____

Lesson 4: Sacred

For each of the aspects of holiness discussed to this point, we've seen clear actions to take when we relate to something or someone as holy—by showing devotion, reverence, and respect. In this last definition of *holy*, we simply see the word *sacred*.[42]

What actions can we take to relate to something as if it's sacred? That all depends on the nature of that "something." Items we find sacred hold special and irreplaceable value to us, so we treat them with care and make sure they're not destroyed.

Is God someone we should relate to as sacred and with that same irreplaceable mentality? What about him is sacred?

> *The LORD answered, "I will make all my splendor pass before you and in your presence I will pronounce my sacred name. I am the LORD, and I show compassion and pity on those I choose." Exodus 33:19*

---

42 *Merriam-Webster's Dictionary and Thesaurus,* Updated Edition, s.v. "Holy."

What do you think God's name being sacred says about God's character?

_____

_____

_____

_____

If we fast forward to the New Testament, we see Jesus relate to God's name as sacred.

> *"This, then, is how you should pray: "'Our Father in heaven, hallowed be your name, your kingdom come, your will be done, on earth as it is in heaven.'"" Matthew 6:9–10 NIV*

While Jesus teaches us how to pray here, the first thing he does is refer to God's name as "hallowed," or in other words, *sacred.*[43]

Why do you think Jesus starts his prayer by first acknowledging that God's name is sacred?

_____

_____

_____

_____

Jesus placed a high value in prayer in his time on earth, and he often retreated to pray and communicate with God. The verses above are the start of him showing us how to communicate with God too. What makes prayer so important, and why did Jesus make sure to communicate with God regularly? Jesus came to earth, died for our sin, and ultimately gave *us* a way to reconcile our relationship with God. What kind of relationship exists without communication? None. Jesus wasted no time in recognizing God's holiness, and if we continue reading his model for prayer, we get a picture of how to communicate with a holy God.

---

43 *Merriam-Webster's Dictionary and Thesaurus,* Updated Edition, s.v. "Hallowed."

"Give us today our daily bread. And forgive us our debts, as we also have forgiven our debtors. And lead us not into temptation, but deliver us from the evil one." Matthew 6:11–13 NIV

Growing up in a Lutheran church, this passage was read every week. I could've recited these verses to you in my sleep as a kid, but telling you what they meant was a whole different story. Knowing and understanding are two vastly different concepts. What is Jesus telling us here in this prayer?

First, Jesus asks God for *provision*. When it comes to reasons why someone would pray, praying for provision is a reason humans can somewhat easily see a need for. We know that we all have needs. We also know that individually, none of us can provide for the needs of all. Jesus didn't just pray for any need, though; he prayed to God for *daily bread*.

Praying for daily bread may not seem significant at first glance, but often times, when we pray to God, we do so in a big-picture aspect. Does that mean that praying for big-picture kinds of provision is a bad thing? Certainly not, but it can be if we write God off as someone who doesn't provide for us because we're only looking for a big-picture answer in return. God regularly answers those big prayers we have by repeatedly providing for our daily bread, not *just* by providing a one-time grand miracle.

If you're like me and know that patience isn't a fruit of the Spirit that you claim to be an expert in, this part of the prayer likely isn't your favorite. Of course, God already knew this about me and tested me in it regularly during my journey to becoming an author. I wanted answers about what this was all really for, and he provided the strength to keep writing, one lesson, one day, at a time. I originally thought I finished with the writing I committed myself to after I completed my first draft nine months later. Oh, how wrong I was!

I didn't get the answer I was seeking in what this writing was all for. Instead, I got the feedback from my writing coach that just when I thought I was "done," I was really just getting started. This was the closest thing to a long-term answer from God that I had received yet. The feedback meant having to include more content and add my story in my book, nearly doubling the original wordcount in the process. I knew this wasn't going to be easy. However, if something is worth doing, it is worth doing right, so I started down this longer path to completion.

What do you need provision for, and how can you pray for God to be that provision?

_____

_____

_____

_____

Next in his prayer, Jesus makes a request for _forgiveness_. Again, this is an ask that, at face value, we could all agree that we need. Regardless of whether we admit it, we all know we aren't perfect—we all need forgiveness, and that's okay! God _wants_ to forgive us, or he would have never sent us Jesus.

The request Jesus makes in this prayer isn't just asking for forgiveness, though; he asks God to forgive us "as we have also forgiven our debtors." What does that mean? It means that we've already extended forgiveness to others before asking for our debts to be forgiven.

To the human heart, this concept sounds backwards, but to a God who sacrificed his Son to forgive our sins while we kept on sinning, it's perfectly fitting.

Who is someone you need to forgive, and why?

_____

_____

_____

_____

Lastly, Jesus asks for _direction_—to be led away from temptation and delivered from evil. God would never tempt us into anything that leads to sin, as he does not want to be separated from us. This means that if we take the directions God gives us, temptation to sin will not be in the blueprint. The schemes of the evil one cannot overcome the holiness of God, nor will they ever be able to. Satan may not be able to see God as worthy of absolute devotion, but that's his loss, because God is only for our good and he cares for us accordingly.

What is something you need to be delivered from, and why?

_____

_____

_____

_____

Dear God,

I confess that I do not always relate to you as being holy and worthy of my absolute devotion. Thank you for being a God who is always loyal, faithful, and constant, even when I'm not. You are the only source in whom I can place my devotion and find complete satisfaction, and that truth alone speaks to your holiness. Help me to overcome the temptation in this world so that I may be obedient and live my life in reverence for you. When I have reverence for you, you bless me in ways that this world will never be able to in the forms of wisdom, life, confidence, and security. Thank you for offering me forgiveness for my sin by paying the price of my sin for me. It is in you alone that I find true life. With your power, I am able to overcome all evil, because the schemes of evil will never overcome your holiness.

In Jesus' name,
Amen.

Chapter Nine

GOD IS HOPE

Lesson 1: Trust

If you've ever been to any kind of camp, retreat, or seminar that involved team-building activities, you may have done an activity called the *trust fall*. A trust fall happens when one person stands with their back facing a group of people. The person then purposefully falls backward, trusting in the people behind to catch them before hitting the ground. If you were asked to be the person who takes the fall, would you do it? Your answer to that question likely depends on who stands in that group of people behind you. Agreeing to take a trust fall becomes a lot easier when it's a group of your best friends behind you versus a group of strangers.

Anytime people make a trust fall, they also place *hope* in the group of people behind them—hoping that they get caught. Once people place their hope in the group and start to fall, they can't *undo* their action of falling. While this is just one example of exercising hope, the act of placing our hope in something in this life holds great power and we need to be mindful of where we place ours.

What is something you have hope for or have placed your hope in recently, and what action did you take as a result of your hope?

_____

_____

_____

_____

When is a time you placed your hope in something and it either failed you or never happened? How did that make you feel?

_____

_____

_____

_____

> **Hope:** _noun_ trust; reliance; desire accompanied by expectation of fulfillment; one that gives promise for the future[44]

One of the places we can place both our trust and hope is in God. God's word declares that God is a God of hope.

> _May the God of hope fill you with all joy and peace as you trust in him,_
> _so that you may overflow with hope by the power of the Holy Spirit._
> _Romans 15:13 NIV_

This verse confirms the correlation between hope and trust, but is God a good choice in whom to place our hope? To answer that, we must first determine whether or not we can trust God. We see that as a result of trusting God, we become filled with joy and peace, but what exactly makes God trustworthy?

---

44 _Merriam-Webster's Dictionary and Thesaurus,_ Updated Edition, s.v. "Hope."

Have you ever experienced being filled with joy and peace as a result of trusting God? If so, when, and what did that joy and peace allow you to do?

_____

_____

_____

_____

  Trust: *noun* one in which confidence is placed[45]

The more we get to know God's character, the more confidence, or trust, we can place in him. Placing our trust and confidence in something puts us in a vulnerable place with whatever we place our trust in. Because of that, we like to know ahead of time whether or not it's really worth it to place our trust in something. Why can we trust God?

> *In my distress I called to the LORD; he answered me and set me free.*
> *The LORD is with me, I will not be afraid; what can anyone do to me?*
> *It is the LORD who helps me, and I will see my enemies defeated. It*
> *is better to trust in the LORD than to depend on people. It is better to*
> *trust in the LORD than to depend on human leaders. Many enemies*
> *were around me; but I destroyed them by the power of the LORD!*
> *Psalm 118:5–10*

The longer I pursued both a career at my day job and whatever calling God had for me as an author, the more clearly I saw these verses play out before me. I had enemies in both pursuits who attempted to destroy my efforts, but the sources in which I placed my trust at both pursuits varied greatly. For my day job, I placed my trust mainly in myself to be able to find the right answer. As I approached two years of working this career, it got to be rather exhausting. I had yet to find the clarity for which I was looking. No matter how hard I tried to do good work, it never seemed to be enough.

Getting frustrated with the fact that everything I tried in that job kept failing, I looked to the help of my trusted coworkers. I met one-on-one with multiple

---

45 *Merriam-Webster.com*, s.v. "Trust," accessed December 04, 2022, https://www.merriam-webster.com/

coworkers close to me, seeking their advice. When I did, it became evident to me that no one else experienced the same difficulties that I did. Rather than seeing my enemies defeated, *I* felt defeated. What was I doing wrong? I went to God about my job situation—more because I wanted answers to the question of what I was doing wrong, not because I wanted to surrender my trust for my career over to him.

Placing trust and confidence in God for my writing came much easier. I would've never entered that path had I not felt like God called me to it. Since I had little confidence in myself to succeed on that path, I placed confidence in God instead.

Despite the shift in where I placed my trust, I was not immune to feelings of failure. I feel like I'm not doing things right at times as an author even today, but the difference is that with God's power, I can and do destroy those enemies who provoke feelings of failure. No enemy we face on this earth has power over God. God is always there for us to call on him, and he always answers. Fear has no place in the presence of God; in him we stand victorious.

What human can promise the freedom, peace, and victory that God provides? None. Only God can provide those results, and he alone deserves our trust.

Where do you find yourself struggling to trust in God?

_____

_____

_____

_____

Have you ever called on God in a time of distress? If so, when, and how did he help you?

_____

_____

_____

_____

Lesson 2: Reliance

Who is someone you rely on? For what do you rely on that person?

_____

_____

_____

_____

The minute we are born into this world, we enter a world of complete reliance. A newborn baby does not possess the knowledge, skills, or resources necessary to keep themselves alive. Babies know they have needs, and they cry to communicate when those needs aren't being met. They _rely_ on someone else to meet all of their needs for them. Without even knowing it, babies place _hope_ in those who hear their cries, because if their cries go unheard, they remain hungry or in need of a diaper change.

As we get older, the reasons for our reliance evolve, and we gain the ability to more consciously choose where or in what we place our hope. When we submit a job application, we hope we get an interview, and to get that interview we rely on someone from the company to reach out to us. Any time we play a team sport, we rely on each person on our team to play their position with the hope of coming away with a victory.

Who or what was the last person or thing you relied on? Did the result of your reliance go as you had hoped? Why or why not?

_____

_____

_____

_____

With my exhaustion and frustration at work reaching an all-time high and the writing of my first book nearing completion, I desperately needed a break from what my life had become over those last two years. I placed hope that a trip to eSwatini, Africa that I had coming up would give me just that. Surely being removed from my daily routine and having a couple of weeks to do nothing but focus on serving God would do the trick. I still had a lot of work to do both in my day job and in writing my book, but I made it a goal to finish all of it at both places and be free from my prior responsibilities before getting on that plane in a short couple of months.

We all have plenty of options for people and things we can rely on surrounding us each day, which makes it easy to not consider God when choosing what to rely on or hope in. Is it wise to leave God out of the conversation, though?

> *Trust in the LORD with all your heart. Never rely on what you think you know. Remember the LORD in everything you do, and he will show you the right way. Never let yourself think that you are wiser than you are; simply obey the LORD and refuse to do wrong. If you do, it will be like good medicine, healing your wounds and easing your pains. Proverbs 3:5–8*

Each verse in that passage addresses a different aspect of how or why we should place our hope in God. God is trustworthy, his knowledge surpasses our understanding, and he can show us the right way. He heals our wounds and eases our pains.

When was a time you placed your hope in God? How did he show you the right way, heal your wounds, or ease your pains as a result?

_____

_____

_____

_____

How do we get to a place where we actively place our hope in God? We have to stop pretending that either we or something else in the world can provide those same qualities that God alone possesses. The moment we start to think anything or anyone else either knows the right way or can show us the right way is the same moment that we place our hope in that person or thing instead of placing our hope in God.

With all of those qualities, one would think that placing our hope in God is a no-brainer. Yet, all of us at times place our hope elsewhere instead. What we rely on and where we place our hope directly reflects what we place our faith in.

Understand, then, that those who have faith are children of Abraham. Scripture foresaw that God would justify the Gentiles by faith, and announced the gospel in advance to Abraham: "All nations will be blessed through you." So those who rely on faith are blessed along with Abraham, the man of faith. For all who rely on the works of the law are under a curse, as it is written: "Cursed is everyone who does not continue to do everything written in the Book of the Law." Clearly no one who relies on the law is justified before God, because "the righteous will live by faith." The law is not based on faith; on the contrary, it says, "The person who does these things will live by them." Christ redeemed us from the curse of the law by becoming a curse for us, for it is written: "Cursed is everyone who is hung on a pole." Galatians 3:7–13 NIV

This passage shows us the difference in results between living a life where we rely on God versus relying on our own works. We are cursed when we rely on our own works because none of us continue to do everything written in the Book of the Law. For as long as we continue to rely on our works, being subject to that curse is our destiny. God, being the redeemer he is, wants to give us an answer for hope in response to that curse and instead asks us to rely on him.

Jesus took on the punishment for our curse by being hung on a pole and crucified for our failure to do everything written in the Book of the Law. By relying on our faith and placing our hope in Jesus, we are blessed and redeemed from our curse. No other source for hope provides us with the same kind of blessing, and the only thing we need to do to receive it is to have faith and believe in Jesus.

When was a time that you relied on your own works? What was the result?

_____

_____

_____

_____

When was a time that you relied on your faith in God? What was the result?

~~

Lesson 3: Fulfillment

The world we live in feeds off of results and productivity. It desires profit and hopes to accomplish as much work with as little time and expense as possible. Although there's nothing inherently wrong with wanting to be productive or profitable, things go very wrong when we put that hope in the wrong place. Hope in this context is described as "desire accompanied by expectation of fulfillment."

Any business owner desires profitability and hopes that their business will succeed. Where this desire becomes unhealthy comes from what expectations for fulfillment a business owner develops to achieve that desire.

What is a desire you have, and what expectations of fulfillment have you made to accomplish that desire?

My desire to finish my book and have it submitted to a professional in the writing industry before going to Africa came quickly. As I sat in my cubicle on the Friday before leaving for Africa, my unsettlement of being there overwhelmed me within just a couple of hours. I knew I wasn't supposed to be there. Halfway through the workday, I decided to listen to the promptings. I took a few hours of personal time and left.

That same day, there was a writing conference going on that was hosted by my writing coach. I had gone to a similar conference before and had people already interested in reading my book once it was done, so I made no plans to go to this one. I intended to fulfill my desire of having my book out of my hands before Africa by contacting someone that I already knew and who had expressed prior interest in my books.

I hadn't entertained the idea of possibly going a different route and sending my book to someone else, but God had different ideas and told me I needed to go to that conference. Sending my book to someone who had already expressed interest in reading it would allow me to fulfill my desire of wanting my book out by a certain deadline more easily—but God isn't exactly a fan of us running our lives on our own timeline.

The more we allow our desires to consume us, the more we set expectations on ourselves to fulfill those desires, and the more likely we are to not fulfill those expectations. If we allow human desires to control our lives and our expectations remain unfulfilled, we begin to find ourselves in a place of hopelessness.

Have you ever felt hopeless because of unfulfilled desires? If so, when, and what did you do as a result?

_____

_____

_____

_____

God hates seeing us in states of hopelessness, and he wants to provide us with a source for hope. Like us, God has desires, but his desires look far different from ours.

> So I say, walk by the Spirit, and you will not gratify the desires of the flesh. For the flesh desires what is contrary to the Spirit, and the Spirit what is contrary to the flesh. They are in conflict with each other, so that you are not to do whatever you want. But if you are led by the Spirit, you are not under the law. Galatians 5:16–18 NIV

As soon as I made it to the writer's conference after leaving work, God showed me just how his desires were different from mine. The second I walked in the door during the middle of one of the sessions, people were in a panic because one of the writing professionals coming to the conference needed a ride from the airport, and no one was available to provide the ride.

Walking into this conference with no intention of attending the conference itself, I volunteered to get the person at the airport, and I quickly found myself leaving on that errand. We had a great conversation all about my book on the way back. I explained that I was going to Africa in just a couple of days and confessed my goal to have my book done by then. Thinking nothing of it, I dropped them off and enjoyed the next day and a half at the conference and away from my cubicle.

At the very end of the conference, I was asked a question I'll never forget. The person I picked up at the airport said to me, "Are you going to pitch your book to me, or do you think you already did during our car ride?" To be honest, I asked myself the same question in my head, but I was too afraid to say it out loud. God made it clear to me in that moment exactly who I needed to send my book to, and it wasn't the person I originally thought.

The desires of God's Spirit differ greatly from the desires of our flesh. After noting this difference in his letter to the Galatians, Paul makes the statement that when the Spirit leads us, we are not under the law. What makes that detail important? To understand its importance, we must be aware of God's desires. God shows us his desires from the very beginning in his first words to mankind.

> *The LORD God took the man and put him in the Garden of Eden to work it and take care of it. And the LORD God commanded the man, "You are free to eat from any tree in the garden; but you must not eat from the tree of the knowledge of good and evil, for when you eat from it you will certainly die." The LORD God said, "It is not good for the man to be alone. I will make a helper suitable for him."*
> *Genesis 2:15–18 NIV*

Here we see God express three key desires—freedom, life, and community. God tells Adam that he is *free* to eat from any tree in the garden. He then warns Adam that even though he has that freedom, not to eat from the tree of the knowledge of good and evil because if he does, he will *die*. God wanted Adam to live, and he didn't want Adam to live *alone*, so he made Eve.

When we live a life focused on the desires of our flesh, we sin. If we do not surrender our life to God and the hope he provides, we remain under the law. Rather than having the freedom, life, and community God desires, we subject ourselves to the consequences of our sin and become:

> <u>Slaves</u>: *Jesus said to them, "I am telling you the truth: everyone who sins is a slave of sin. A slave does not belong to a family permanently, but a son belongs there forever. If the Son sets you free, then you will be really free." John 8:34–36*
>
> <u>Dead</u>: *For the wages of sin is death, but the gift of God is eternal life in Christ Jesus our Lord. Romans 6:23 NIV*
>
> <u>Separated</u>: *It is because of your sins that he doesn't hear you. It is your sins that separate you from God when you try to worship him. Isaiah 59:2*

How has your sin made you feel like a slave, dead, or separated from God?

_____

_____

_____

_____

God knows that we all sin and cannot fulfill his desires for us to be full of freedom, life, and in community. The good news for us? He doesn't place the expectation, or *hope*, on us to become people who can fulfill those desires—he knows we can't do it. Instead, he sent Jesus to be a fulfillment of the law for us.

> *"Do not think that I have come to abolish the Law or the Prophets; I have not come to abolish them but to fulfill them." Matthew 5:17 NIV*

Jesus took on the wage of death for us and fulfilled the Law by living a sinless life. When we place our hope and faith in Jesus's death for our sin, we receive God's Spirit. The Holy Spirit shares God's desires, and when we possess it, God restores our freedom, life, and community with him. We are free from the wages of sin and have eternal life with Christ Jesus in heaven. Jesus is our only hope to receive that freedom, life, and community with God, and God desires for us to have it so badly, he offers it freely to all who will accept his invitation.

Why do you think Jesus makes it a point to acknowledge that he didn't come to abolish the Law, but to fulfill it?

_____

_____

_____

_____

How have you placed your hope in God? What freedom, life, or community did you receive as a result?

_____

_____

_____

_____

Lesson 4: Promises

If I'm being honest, I'm not much of a fan of this lesson's topic in a "worldly" sense. Why? Because as humans, we're not historically great at living up to our promises. At my core, I'm a very action-driven and results-oriented person. Those qualities carry a lot of benefit when it comes to things like my love for research, but they don't carry as much benefit when it comes to someone promising me that they're going to do something. My rebel-like tendencies don't help in improving my relationship with promises either—I've never been much of one to do something just because someone expected me to do it. If I'm driven to do something, I'll do it, and I don't need to be promised a certain result in order to start acting.

Part of my dislike for promises in a worldly context comes from how promises relate to being a source for _hope_, as seen in the definition, "one that gives promise for the future." Our world recognizes the importance of having this kind of hope, and it does what it can to find solutions that give promise for the future.

Nearly every consumer-driven business turns to predictive analytics and hires data analysts for the sole purpose of those analysts providing them with reports that give them hope for their business's future. I know this well because I used to be one of those analysts. Although I enjoyed what I did in that season of my life, I couldn't claim to be an expert at providing that kind of hope. That wasn't because I didn't know how to do my job well, but because the uncertainty of providing hope using predictive analytics is in the name itself—they're *predictions*, not promises.

What was the last promise someone made to you? Did their promise bring you any hope? Why or why not?

_____

_____

_____

_____

I loved the type of work I did as a data analyst, but as far as a career was concerned, God had other plans for my life. I successfully accomplished my goals of submitting my book to a professional and completing my work projects before going to Africa for two weeks. Upon my return, God wasted no time in throwing another curveball my way. My career as a data analyst ended less than a week after I came back from that mission trip. Completely taken aback from having so much of the life I worked toward for years gone just like that, I cried for a week straight while asking God, "Why?!"

The world can try as much as it likes, but it cannot make promises that last. For better or for worse, I saw this concept playing out first-hand in my life. What would my career look like from here? I had no clue, but I did know that drastic changes were in store for my near future.

Unlike the world's promises, I love promises from God. God doesn't need to hire anyone to help him make predictions for the future. He already *knows* what the future holds.

When my bones were being formed, carefully put together in my mother's womb, when I was growing there in secret, you knew that I was there— you saw me before I was born. The days allotted to me had all been recorded in your book, before any of them ever began. Psalm 139:15–16

God made the plan for each of our lives before our lives even began. He's well aware of what is happening and what is going to happen. What does this mean when we consider God as a source of hope? It means that God is the *ultimate* source of hope. When God makes a promise for the future, it happens one hundred percent of the time, because he already knows it's going to happen. The question isn't *if* God is a reliable source of hope; the question is what God promises when we place our hope in him.

If we say that we have no sin, we deceive ourselves, and there is no truth in us. But if we confess our sins to God, he will keep his promise and do what is right: he will forgive us our sins and purify us from all our wrongdoing. 1 John 1:8–9

Why is the promise God makes in these verses important, and how does it give you hope?

_____

_____

_____

_____

The fact that God forgives us and purifies us of our wrongdoing is incredible, but the goodness and hope of God doesn't stop there. God not only makes this great promise to us, but his promise also gives us hope for the future. What does that future hold?

I consider that what we suffer at this present time cannot be compared at all with the glory that is going to be revealed to us. All of creation waits with eager longing for God to reveal his children. For creation was condemned to lose its purpose, not of its own will, but because God willed it to be so. Yet there was hope that creation itself would one day be set free from its slavery to decay and would share the glorious freedom of the children of God. For we know that up to the present time all of creation groans with pain, like the pain of childbirth. But it is not just creation alone which groans; we who have the Spirit as the first of God's gifts also groan within ourselves as we wait for God to make us his children and set our whole being free. For it was by hope that we were saved; but if we see what we hope for, then it is not really hope. For who of us hopes for something we see? Romans 8:18–24

What do you think the phrase "it was by hope that we were saved" means, and how have you been saved by hope?

_____

_____

_____

_____

The future that God offers through his promise to forgive us and purify us of our sin is a future of freedom. Without God's hope, we remain bound to the slavery of sin. God doesn't want to just set part of our life free; he wants to set our whole being free. By his hope, we are saved. We may not see the promise God offers us now, but if we could see it, we wouldn't need his hope. We don't need to physically see God's promises, we just need to place our faith in God and in the fact that he knows what he's doing. Our hope in him results in a freedom unlike the freedom anyone or anything else can offer.

Has the presence of hope allowed you to endure trials on this earth? If so, how?

_____

_____

_____

_____

Where do you find yourself struggling to place your hope in God, and why?

_____

_____

_____

_____

Dear God,

I come to you now and place my trust in you. You are the only source in whom I can place my trust and always experience joy and peace as a result. You are a God of hope, and by the power of your Spirit I can overflow with hope. I have no reason to fear anything on this earth, because I can depend on you, and in my distress, you set me free. Show me where I am relying on myself to know the right way, and help me surrender those thoughts to you, because you are the way. You are a God of fulfillment, and you desire a life for me that is full of freedom and centered in a relationship with you. You knew me when I was being knit together in my mother's womb, and you know what my future holds. Thank you for being a God who never makes a promise that you won't keep, and for being someone who is available at all times for me to approach and place my hope in.

In Jesus' name,
Amen.

GOD IS SOVEREIGN

Lesson 1: Supreme

With most of the chapters in this book, it's easy for one to see the good in someone or something that possesses those qualities. Who doesn't want to associate with someone who is kind, full of hope, and marvelous? Depending on the nature of the sovereignty, the outcome of someone being sovereign could be great, but it could also be terrible.

Sovereign: *adjective* supreme in power or authority; having undisputed ascendency; chief; having independent authority[46]

Being sovereign doesn't just mean one has power; it means they are *supreme* in power. The outcome of one's sovereignty depends on how that power is utilized. Because of the possibility for such vast differences in outcomes as a result of something being sovereign, it is important to know the one who is sovereign. That sovereignty and being supreme in power has an extreme impact on each of us who are *not* sovereign.

Before getting too deep into this chapter, we must first address the question: is God sovereign? If so, how does he use his power and authority?

"Sovereign LORD, you made the earth and the sky by your great power and might; nothing is too difficult for you." Jeremiah 32:17

---

46   *Merriam-Webster's Dictionary and Thesaurus,* Updated Edition, s.v. "Sovereign."

When was a time that something seemed too difficult for you? What did you do as a result of determining it to be too difficult?

_____

_____

_____

_____

When things get difficult in your life, do you surrender them to God? Why or why not?

_____

_____

_____

_____

Jeremiah addresses God as being sovereign, and he tells us that God created the earth and the sky through his sovereignty. Because of God's great power, nothing is too difficult for him. That quality alone sets God apart from each of us—we have all encountered times in life where things got difficult. We are not sovereign, and our own power comes nowhere close to being supreme.

Being let go from my job that I worked so hard to succeed in showed me first-hand my lack of power and authority. How did it make me feel? I felt like a complete failure. Did that mean I was actually a failure? Of course not. Viewing myself as a failure came naturally when placing the blame for what happened on myself. In reality, I took ownership for things that weren't my fault, what happened was outside of my control or authority.

While we do not possess that great of power or authority, the Bible says that God does possess that power. Is it a good thing that God is supreme in power? That all depends on how God chooses to exercise his sovereignty—for what God uses his power.

> _Praise be to the Lord, to God our Savior, who daily bears our burdens._
> _Our God is a God who saves; from the Sovereign LORD comes escape_
> _from death. Psalm 68:19–20 NIV_

What has God saved you from, and what impact did that have on you?

_____

_____

_____

_____

Out of everything for which God could use his sovereignty, he uses it to provide us with an *escape from death*. Death was never God's intention for us. He cautioned humanity from the very beginning with what would lead them to death and how to avoid it.

> *And the LORD God commanded the man, "You are free to eat from any tree in the garden; but you must not eat from the tree of the knowledge of good and evil, for when you eat from it you will certainly die."*
> *Genesis 2:16–17 NIV*

Adam and Eve didn't listen to God. Instead, they ate from the tree and sinned. As a result of their sin, they earned death—the same death we all still earn today as a result of our sin.

God knows we have all earned our death, but our sin does not change God's love for us and his desire for us to live rather than die. In order for us to not die, God had to use his sovereignty to provide us with an escape from death. Overcoming death is too difficult for us, but it's not too difficult for God.

> *"Fellow Israelites, listen to this: Jesus of Nazareth was a man accredited by God to you by miracles, wonders and signs, which God did among you through him, as you yourselves know. This man was handed over to you by God's deliberate plan and foreknowledge; and you, with the help of wicked men, put him to death by nailing him to the cross. But God raised him from the dead, freeing him from the agony of death, because it was impossible for death to keep its hold on him."*
> *Acts 2:22–24 NIV*

Death never stood a chance against a God who is supreme in power. God didn't just use his miraculous power to raise Jesus from the dead; he extends that same power to us through his Holy Spirit.

For the Spirit God gave us does not make us timid, but gives us power, love and self-discipline. So do not be ashamed of the testimony about our Lord or of me his prisoner. Rather, join with me in suffering for the gospel, by the power of God. He has saved us and called us to a holy life—not because of anything we have done but because of his own purpose and grace. This grace was given us in Christ Jesus before the beginning of time, but it has now been revealed through the appearing of our Savior, Christ Jesus, who has destroyed death and has brought life and immortality to light through the gospel. 2 Timothy 1:7–10 NIV

God loves us too much to allow shame, timidity, and death rule over our lives. His power gives us an answer to overcome them all. God doesn't do this for us because he felt like he *had* to; this extension of grace was in God's plan from the very *beginning*. From this grace, we gain access to the life and freedom found in Christ.

I can't say that being let go from my job gave me this overwhelming sense of life and freedom, but I didn't want to let circumstances outside of my control be the lord over my life, either. The pain it caused and the tears that flowed were real, but so is the God who was calling me to greater things now that this job was no longer part of my life. Not having a job gave me freedom in my day-to-day schedule.

I suddenly found myself with a lot of time I didn't previously have, along with the freedom to choose how I spent that time. As we see in the Timothy passage, I had two options of how to spend my new free time—I could either sit there and be ashamed of both my testimony and the fact that I couldn't find a way to make things work at my job, or I could spend my time living for the gospel.

Upon making the choice to live for the gospel, the very next week I took my first serious step toward living my life as an advocate for sexual assault survivors. I knew I was sharing my own story as a survivor in my writing, and while my first book hadn't yet come out, I knew I needed to get more involved in that space. God gave me the power to write my story in my books, and I knew he'd give me the power to do this too.

Where is timidity present in your life? How could God's power help you overcome that timidity?

_____

_____

_____

_____

What life is God calling you to? Do you see God's power present in that calling? If so, how?

_____

_____

_____

_____

～

Lesson 2: Ascendency

As someone who grew up in the Midwest, I spent many nights of my childhood playing various card games—a favorite of mine being euchre. Game nights often quickly become competitive, and it's inevitable that at some point during the night, two people will disagree over a ruling in the game.

Many games have certain aspects that people play multiple different ways, and the group must decide which rules to play. The question is, who gets to make that decision? Usually, this decision gets made by the host of the game night— their house, their rules.

By following "house rules" at a game night, we grant the type of sovereignty defined as "having undisputed ascendency" to the person who lives in that house.

Ascendancy: _noun_ controlling influence[47]

---

47   _Merriam-Webster's Dictionary and Thesaurus,_ Updated Edition, s.v. "Ascendency."

In the case of game night, the governing or controlling influence is the homeowner setting the rules. What makes following house rules also undisputable is the fact that the other people playing can't fake that they live in that house.

Sovereignty in this context brings clarity to how decisions will be made at a game night, but is this kind of sovereignty also necessary in our world as a whole? I think it is. Consider this: if we need to have one governing influence over something as small as a game night to keep peace, how much more necessary is it to have one undisputed governing authority in our world as a whole?

Do you think it's a good thing for our world to have an undisputed governing influence? Why or why not?

_____

_____

_____

_____

If God is the answer to this kind of sovereignty in our world, he must first have a governing or controlling influence over the whole world. Does God have this kind of power, and if so, what does that power look like?

> There in front of the whole assembly, King David praised the LORD.
> He said, "LORD God of our ancestor Jacob, may you be praised forever
> and ever! You are great and powerful, glorious, splendid, and majestic.
> Everything in heaven and earth is yours, and you are king, supreme
> ruler over all. All riches and wealth come from you; you rule everything
> by your strength and power; and you are able to make anyone great
> and strong." 1 Chronicles 29:10–12

David declares in these verses that God does indeed have ruling, or governing, influence over all of heaven and earth by means of his strength and power. God is great, glorious, splendid, majestic, and able to make each of us great and strong too. This is great news for each of us because we are powerless when ruled, or influenced, by our sin.

*For what the law was powerless to do because it was weakened by the
flesh, God did by sending his own Son in the likeness of sinful flesh
to be a sin offering. And so he condemned sin in the flesh, in order
that the righteous requirement of the law might be fully met in us,
who do not live according to the flesh but according to the Spirit.*
Romans 8:3–4 NIV

It is only by God's strength that I pushed through this next season of life as I
figured out where my career would go next. I had a narrow vision of the path God
placed me on, but God's influence stayed evident in my writing journey. Sitting
in the middle of this season of joblessness and waiting to hear back from the pub-
lisher on whether my book would be accepted for publication, I began investing
in my future by establishing my own business as an author. As someone who has a
master's degree in business, one would think that this came easily. I wish it would
have, but a lot of the classes in schools only prepare people for the skills they need
to succeed in corporate America.

**How do you think our world would look different if it actually related to God
as king and ruler over it all?**

_____

_____

_____

_____

**Has God made you great and strong in any way? If so, how? If not, how could
you use his greatness and strength?**

_____

_____

_____

_____

God's influence governs over our entire world, but in order to be sovereign, his influence must also be undisputed. Can anyone or anything in this world overcome or overtake God's power?

> Shout for joy to God, all the earth! Sing the glory of his name; make his praise glorious. Say to God, "How awesome are your deeds! So great is your power that your enemies cringe before you. All the earth bows down to you; they sing praise to you, they sing the praises of your name." Psalm 66:1–4 NIV

Nothing and no one on this earth will ever come close to matching God's power. His power is so great and sovereign that his enemies *cringe* before him. When we possess God's power through his Holy Spirit, our enemies cringe before us, too. God's power being this great is far from a bad thing—it's actually the greatest news the world could hope for. It is *only* by God's power that we get access to eternal life with him.

> For when you were baptized, you were buried with Christ, and in baptism you were also raised with Christ through your faith in the active power of God, who raised him from death. Colossians 2:12

All of us who receive the Holy Spirit possess this great and active power of God, but do we allow this power to influence our lives and live with authority over the enemies of this world? I'd argue that most of the time, we don't. I'll be the first to admit that I haven't always lived with this level of authority.

My new daily routine in life involved volunteering with other organizations that helped sexual assault survivors, filling out job applications, and trying to figure out how to register for a business. During the time I spent volunteering, I crossed paths with someone who invited me to speak at my first event related to sexual assault awareness. I couldn't say no to such a great opportunity. I accepted the invite, and after speaking at the event, I ended up getting interviewed and featured on the news.

I don't say this to brag, but as an example of how I struggled to live in the authority that the power of the Holy Spirit gives us. I watched that interview on TV and couldn't do anything but cringe. Instead of my enemies cringing before me, I cringed before them, and that couldn't have made Satan any happier! I watched the interview at least ten more times before I became somewhat okay with it. However, I still didn't like it enough to want to post anything about it or share it with others, so I didn't. In reality, all I did by not sharing the interview was interfere with bringing glory to God through the speaking opportunity that he gave me to begin with.

Where do you need to give God more glory in your life?

_____

_____

_____

_____

Knowing that nothing can overpower God, how can you use that knowledge to live with more authority in your life?

_____

_____

_____

_____

Lesson 3: Chief

In this next aspect of sovereignty, we find a definition that simply states *chief*. If someone asked me what first comes to mind when hearing the word *chief*, my response would be "grocery shopping," because the main grocery store in my small hometown was named Chief. (It was actually pronounced "Chief's," because people in the Midwest love to make things possessive for some reason.) I'm pretty sure grocery shopping has nothing to do with God's sovereignty or being sovereign in general. Instead, let's focus on the following aspect of being chief:

<u>Chief:</u> *adjective* highest in rank[48]

In general, our world *loves* this kind of sovereignty—after all, the higher the rank, the greater the power, right? We love this type of sovereignty so much that we place a ranking system on just about everything we do. Our job titles come with a rank within our company, sports players looking to go pro are ranked as recruits, and authors love to see their books ranked on bestseller lists. Looking for recommendations? There's some sort of "top 10" list for *everything*. If we want to travel somewhere, bake something, watch a movie, or do just about anything else, someone out there has voiced an opinion on their chief recommendations to meet our needs.

What is something in which you have achieved a higher rank, and what benefits did you receive as a result of that rank?

_____

_____

_____

_____

Being chief, or the highest in rank, has its fair share of benefits, or our world wouldn't idolize the concept so much. Anything we assign a rank to has someone or something becoming "chief" as a result of it being the highest of those assigned ranks. We are all familiar with this concept of being chief in a worldly context, but in order for God to be sovereign, this concept of being chief must also be true from a Godly standpoint.

> For the LORD your God is God of gods and Lord of lords, the great God, mighty and awesome, who shows no partiality and accepts no bribes. Deuteronomy 10:17 NIV

In what is God chief, or of highest rank? Simply put, being God. He is the God of gods and the Lord of lords—there are no gods above him and there never

---

48 *Merriam-Webster's Dictionary and Thesaurus,* Updated Edition, s.v. "Chief."

will be. His power, might, and greatness earn him this rank, and because he holds this rank, *we* are the recipients of the benefits.

Have you witnessed the great power and might of God? If so, what did it look like?

_____

_____

_____

_____

In our highly materialistic culture, sometimes our world takes the benefits or gifts we receive for granted because they don't live up to our expectations. The benefits we receive as a result of God's sovereignty are far from something we should take for granted, though. The benefits we gain from God's sovereignty far exceed anything we could come up with on our own.

While the benefits that living a life with God far outweigh anything our world can offer us, we all still struggle to fully surrender our lives to God. Why is that? A big reason is that we love *control*. For me, I hated the uncertainty involved with the direction of my career. Over a span of six months, I applied for a countless number of jobs similar to the one from which I was let go. Second and third interviews came my way regularly, but somehow, I never got a job offer. I kept applying to these jobs because with my education and years of hard work I put into that career, I felt like it was my "duty" to apply for them. I wasn't taking the hint from God that the career I once had no longer applied to my life and that he had other things in store for me.

Think about it: God is the God of gods and the Lord of lords. He is almighty and all-powerful. God could literally do anything he wanted to do with that kind of power, and what does he do? He shows no partiality and accepts no bribes. The essence of his character lies in the fact that God shows no partiality and accepts no bribes—he is fair, just, and doesn't expect any of us to "earn" our way to him.

Why is it important to know that God shows no partiality and accepts no bribes? Does knowing that change how you relate to God? If so, how?

_____

_____

_____

_____

We see in that Deuteronomy verse what God *doesn't* do in the sense of showing partiality and accepting bribes, but what *does* he do instead?

> *He defends the cause of the fatherless and the widow, and loves the foreigner residing among you, giving them food and clothing. Deuteronomy 10:18 NIV*

God holds the power to do anything, and he uses that power to defend, love, and provide for us. He does all of this for our benefit, *not* his own. What other chiefly-ranked thing uses power purely for the benefit of others? None, and that alone makes the fact that God is the God of gods and Lord of lords some of the greatest news our world has ever heard.

Why do you think God uses his sovereignty to defend, love, and provide for others?

_____

_____

_____

_____

How has God defended, loved, or provided for you? what benefit did you receive as a result?

_____

_____

_____

_____

~∽

Lesson 4: Authority

Each day of our lives, starting from the second we wake up, we get faced with a series of decisions. Do we push the snooze button? What do we wear to work? What should we make for dinner? We take no action before first making a decision.

The decisions we choose to make set the tone for our lives and hold a lot of power. However, the decisions we make aren't always just for ourselves. Anyone who manages a group of people makes decisions on behalf of the entire group because they have been given the power, or *authority*, to make those decisions.

> **Authority:** *noun* power to influence or command thought, opinion, or behavior[49]

During those six months of being jobless, I was forced to make many decisions. Some of these decisions were ones I enjoyed making. In this season, I received the official notice that *Broken Lenses: Identifying Your Truth in a World of Lies* got accepted for publication. Making the decision to accept the offer or publication and continue to move down this path of writing God had me on was a no-brainer. Accepting this opportunity led me down a path of many other decisions over which I had authority—from the interior layout of the book to the cover design and the official title. I held influence over every decision that led to my book's final product. In the end, I can say I'm still proud of the result to this day.

What is a decision you made recently? What gave you the power or authority to make that decision, and what impact did that decision have?

_____

_____

_____

_____

---

[49] *Merriam-Webster.com,* s.v. "Authority," accessed December 04, 2022, https://www.merriam-webster.com/

We all make many decisions, and all know at least from a conceptual level that there is power in having the authority to make decisions. Where does that power and authority come from? Being sovereign takes this concept of authority to a different level. In order to be sovereign, simply having authority isn't enough; one must have *independent* authority.

While the world we live in attempts to convince us that we have independent authority to make decisions in our lives, the truth is that we don't. Although we *do* have complete control over the plans we make for our lives, we *do not* have control of the world around us, and the plans we decide to make don't always happen.

> *The heart of man plans his way, but the LORD establishes his steps.*
> Proverbs 16:9 ESV

What is a plan you've made for your life that didn't play out according to plan? What prevented what you had planned from happening?

_____

_____

_____

_____

This verse shows us that while we *do* have authority to plan our lives, we *don't* have the authority to determine the steps of that plan. There are too many external factors that we don't have control of in this world that affect our plan, and therefore our authority becomes *dependent* on something.

Other decisions that I had to make in this time of my life were far from enjoyable. At the end of my six months of joblessness, the money I had saved up from my former job came to its end. I needed an income, and I wasn't succeeding despite all of the applications I filled out. I didn't have the authority to hire myself, and I didn't have the authority to manipulate someone else into changing their mind in hiring me, so I changed course. Exactly what kind of course change did I make? I needed to stop trying to make something of myself and just allow God to continue to grow me into the person he already created me to be.

God made this world by his power, and he alone has the independent authority to make the decision of what happens here.

> *But God made the earth by his power; he founded the world by his wisdom and stretched out the heavens by his understanding. Jeremiah 10:12 NIV*

How does God choose to exhibit this power and authority in order to influence behavior?

> *Then Jesus came to them and said, "All authority in heaven and on earth has been given to me. Therefore go and make disciples of all nations, baptizing them in the name of the Father and of the Son and of the Holy Spirit, and teaching them to obey everything I have commanded you. And surely I am with you always, to the very end of the age. Matthew 28:18–20 NIV*

In this demonstration of authority, we get a clear picture of God's heart. Jesus declares that all authority in heaven and earth has been given to him. He holds the power to influence anything on this earth that he wants to, and he decides to use that authority to give the command to go and make disciples of all nations.

This command shows us God's heart for love, unity, and relationships. Jesus's love for each of us is so vast that even when he had the power to give any command he wanted, he gave us a command solely for our benefit. He wants us to be united and in a relationship with him, and he knows that isn't possible unless we place our faith in him and receive his Holy Spirit. Jesus also loves us all way too much to leave any of us hanging. After giving this command to make disciples, he assures them that he is always there with them—we are never on this journey alone!

Have you accepted Jesus's command to go and make disciples? Why or why not?

_____

_____

_____

_____

What does making disciples mean to you, and how does knowing that God is always with you help in making those disciples?

_____

_____

_____

_____

Dear God,

Thank you for being a God who is capable of all things and for using your supreme power and authority to save my life and provide me with an escape from death. Nothing is too difficult for you, and when I place my faith in you as my Lord and Savior, no trial is too difficult for me to overcome either. Death never stood a chance against you, and it never will. You are a God of love, and you love me too much to allow shame, timidity, or death to have the final say over my life. There is no one above you. You are the God of gods and the Lord of lords. Even though you could use your power for anything, you choose to use your power to defend, love, and provide for me. I confess that I don't always allow you to have authority in my life, and I ask for you to show me the next step in the plan you have for me. Your sovereignty is unmatched, and your goodness is displayed in how you use your sovereign nature to make sure I know that you love me and care for me.

In Jesus' name,
Amen.

Chapter Eleven

GOD IS MIRACULOUS

Lesson 1: Works

One of the biggest lies our world feeds us is the illusion that we can "do it all." When we pair that lie with the lie that getting help somehow makes us "weak," it results in people working night and day to try to live up to and be people they aren't, ultimately getting burned out. The complex that these two lies form causes us to get frustrated. Why? Because, regardless of whether we want to admit it, we all know that we *can't* "do it all."

When we constantly live a life of trying to do something that we already know we can't do, the only thing we're successfully doing is setting ourselves up for failure. I'm not saying any one person is a failure in their identity or nature. God created everyone on this planet, and God does *not* create failures! While none of us is a failure, we do all have limitations, and those limitations result in us not being able to "do it all."

We have all come to a place in life where the situation was outside of our control. In those situations, we may find ourselves looking for a *miracle*. The question is, when we get to that place, where do we go to look for that miracle?

When was a time in your life that you needed a miracle, and why?

_____

_____

_____

_____

Miraculous: *adjective* working or able to work miracles[50]

My seemingly never-ending season of not having a day job came to a point where I needed to get some kind of income, or I wasn't going to be able to pay my next month's rent. I did not see any hope for a change in my job status, and I came to a place of needing a miracle. After spending so much time and energy looking for a new job and having no luck in securing one, feelings of insufficiency became my status quo. Regardless of those feelings of insufficiency, I knew I needed to find something to provide income, so I was not shy in sharing my current state of life and employment needs with those around me.

We can choose to look for a miracle from anyone or in anything we want, but whether that person or thing can actually work a miracle is a different story. Is God able to work miracles?

> *Everything you do, O God, is holy. No god is as great as you. You are the God who works miracles; you showed your might among the nations. Psalm 77:13–14*

Has God worked a miracle in your life? If so, when?

_____

_____

_____

_____

---

50 *Merriam-Webster's Dictionary and Thesaurus,* Updated Edition, s.v. "Miraculous."

The holy and miraculous God that this Psalm speaks of is the same holy and miraculous God we have today. Just like we all have the ability to receive God's Spirit, we all have the ability to be both witnesses and recipients of God's miraculous ways.

> *Tell me this one thing: did you receive God's Spirit by doing what the Law requires or by hearing the gospel and believing it? How can you be so foolish! You began by God's Spirit, do you now want to finish by your own power? Did all your experience mean nothing at all? Surely it meant something! Does God give you the Spirit and work miracles among you because you do what the Law requires or because you hear the gospel and believe it? Consider the experience of Abraham; as the scripture says, "He believed God, and because of his faith God accepted him as righteous." Galatians 3:2–6*

Paul opens this passage by asking a rhetorical question—the Galatians knew full well that they had received God's Spirit by believing in the gospel. The Galatians were no different than us today: having faith and believing in God and his miracle-working ways comes easily when we get to a point in life where circumstances are outside of our control. For the most part, if we're honest with ourselves, we do exactly what the Galatians did and resort to doing things on our own power whenever we feel like we can.

I admittedly tried to do everything in my power to get another job, but at the end of the day, nothing worked. After coming to a point of recognizing that I needed a miracle, God provided that miracle—it just wasn't the miracle I wanted. Knowing that I needed a job, someone I had talked to only a couple of times before came to me and said their work needed help. The catch? It wasn't another analyst job. It was working as a barista at a restaurant for barely more than a minimum hourly wage.

With a master's degree, stepping down from a career to take this job wasn't exactly what I had in mind. Ultimately, I had to remember what was more important. If working this job allowed me to pay my rent next month and still pursue writing, then that was what mattered most. While it was far from the miracle I wanted, it provided those two things, so I accepted the job.

What was the last thing you tried to finish on your own power? What was the result?

_____

_____

_____

_____

Being the one who created us, God _knows_ what we can and can't do. None of us can do what the Law requires on our own strength, but what we all can do in our own strength is _believe_ in something. Whether we believe in God or not, our belief drives every single action we take—or don't take—in life. God's miraculous ways aren't reserved for the people who are "good enough." God works miracles among anyone who believes he is a miracle worker, and we all have the ability to place that belief in him.

Why do you choose to believe in the things that you believe in?

_____

_____

_____

_____

What actions are you taking—or not taking—right now based on your belief in God?

_____

_____

_____

_____

Lesson 2: Manifesting

Life at some point brings us all to a place where we need a miracle. We want something, but we have no idea how to achieve it, so we hope for a miracle instead. I'm going to bet I'm not alone in coming out disappointed when hoping for a miracle at some point because what we wanted to happen didn't happen. But does the fact that our desired result didn't happen mean that we didn't get the miracle we asked for? Not necessarily.

When we come to this place of looking for a miracle, we almost always have a desired result. However, we also know that what happens is outside our control. As humans, we love to be in control, and situations outside our control can quickly become frustrating. We get fixated on searching for the result rather than searching for the miracle. In reality, we've likely had more miracles happen in our lives than we realize. We just didn't notice them.

Have you ever received a miracle you were looking for? If so, when?

_____

_____

_____

_____

In the previous lesson, we discussed that God is able to work miracles, but in order to fully appreciate God's miraculous nature, we're going to dissect what miracles consist of.

> **Miracle:** *noun* an extraordinary event manifesting divine intervention in human affairs[51]

God providing the job opportunity of being a barista when he did proved to me that his divine intervention was at work, but I'd be lying if I said it felt *extraordinary*. I was a twenty-seven-year-old with a master's degree, and I worked as a barista at a restaurant with a fresh-out-of-high-school kid as my boss. To say it felt embarrassing would be an understatement. How on earth did this bring any glory to God?

---

51 *Merriam-Webster's Dictionary and Thesaurus,* Updated Edition, s.v. "Miracle."

One day, a former MBA classmate of mine came into the restaurant. As soon as I noticed them, I hid in the back until they left. I was too ashamed to show my face—man, did Satan *love* that feeling of defeat! When would this so-called miracle ever actually *feel* like a miracle?

For God to be miraculous, he must first be capable of extraordinary events, and the event must *manifest* divine intervention. The gospels give us many examples of the extraordinary events Jesus performed during his time on earth, but were those events miraculous? Did they manifest anything, and if so, what?

> **<u>Manifest:</u>** *verb* to make clear or evident to the eye or the understanding; show plainly[52]

Of all the extraordinary events Jesus did in his time on earth, none of them were ever just for his own benefit. Jesus came to *serve*, not to *be served*. By being focused on others, his actions made God's character manifest—or clear and evident—to many.

Why is knowing this important? Because God moves in each of our lives just as he did in Jesus's life. The miracles that God works in our lives are *not* meant to be for the benefit of just ourselves! The miracles God worked in my life and career didn't feel like miracles because I only looked at them from the perspective of my own life. If all I could ever think about was the embarrassment I felt while working this new job, it would never feel like a miracle. The truth is that God did so much more in my life than I could comprehend; I just needed to quit being narrow-minded.

Has God shown himself to you? If so, what was it that he made clear or evident?

_____

_____

_____

_____

---

52 *Dictionary.com*, s.v. "Manifest," accessed December 04, 2022, https://www.dictionary.com/

During his ministry on earth, Jesus performed many miracles, and we see in the first miracle that he performed what those miracles manifested:

On the third day there was a wedding at Cana in Galilee, and the mother of Jesus was there. Jesus also was invited to the wedding with his disciples. When the wine ran out, the mother of Jesus said to him, "They have no wine." And Jesus said to her, "Woman, what does this have to do with me? My hour has not yet come." His mother said to the servants, "Do whatever he tells you." Now there were six stone water jars there for the Jewish rites of purification, each holding twenty or thirty gallons. Jesus said to the servants, "Fill the jars with water." And they filled them up to the brim. And he said to them, "Now draw some out and take it to the master of the feast." So they took it. When the master of the feast tasted the water now become wine, and did not know where it came from (though the servants who had drawn the water knew), the master of the feast called the bridegroom and said to him, "Everyone serves the good wine first, and when people have drunk freely, then the poor wine. But you have kept the good wine until now." This, the first of his signs, Jesus did at Cana in Galilee, and manifested his glory. And his disciples believed in him.
John 2:1–11 ESV

Why do you think the master made it a point to say that what they served him was good wine?

_____

_____

_____

_____

This passage shows us God's power at work and what happens when we stay open and willing to receive his miracle-working ways. Jesus attends a wedding with his disciples, and they run out of wine. In an effort to replenish the wine, Jesus's mother wisely instructs the disciples to do whatever Jesus says, and they do just that. They fill the large jars with water, and when they draw some liquid out of the jar, they find that they no longer have water, but wine.

As they bring the wine to the master of the feast, we see two different reactions take place. The master of the feast tastes the wine and simply comments on the quality of the wine, not knowing where it came from but nonetheless appreciating its taste. However, the servants who drew the water *did* know where the wine came from. They knew that an extraordinary event had just taken place, and Jesus made his miracle-working ways evident to them, manifesting his glory.

The people at this wedding all had a desired result—they had run out of wine and wanted to replenish it. They also knew that replenishing the wine was out of their control. Knowing that wine comes from grapes, I'm going to assume that turning water into wine wasn't how they thought the miracle would get answered. However, they didn't keep their minds narrowed into getting frustrated while looking for an answer. They surrendered the situation to Jesus, listened to what he told them to do, and as a result witnessed a miracle.

What is something in your life that you need to surrender?

_____

_____

_____

_____

What is something you have previously surrendered? Did you see God's glory displayed as a result?

_____

_____

_____

_____

Lesson 3: Divine

Based on the actions each of us take and the decisions each of us make in our daily lives, we manifest results accordingly. If we look to manifest a healthier body, we may decide to start working out more or to eat a more healthy diet. If we look to manifest a career change, we might go back to school or start our own business. We have all seen the impact of what our decisions manifest in our lives, but have we all witnessed a miracle?

To fit under the definition, a miracle cannot manifest just anything. Miracles consist of events that manifest something *divine*. Why is this distinction important? The Bible confirms that as humans, our actions do in fact manifest things, but those things are far from divine.

> *What human nature does is quite plain. It shows itself in immoral, filthy, and indecent actions; in worship of idols and witchcraft. People become enemies and they fight; they become jealous, angry, and ambitious. They separate into parties and groups; they are envious, get drunk, have orgies, and do other things like these. I warn you now as I have before: those who do these things will not possess the Kingdom of God. Galatians 5:19–21*

How have you seen any of the results in the above passage take place in your own life? What actions took place to manifest them?

_____

_____

_____

_____

Even though all of us have been impacted by the jealousy, anger, and separation that manifests from our human nature, I'm willing to bet that none of us enjoyed it. Each of these qualities manifested themselves in my new job regularly if I wasn't mindful enough to keep my mind fixed on what God had in store for me. It was pretty easy for the anger and jealousy associated with human nature to settle in when I was working a job that I was way over-qualified for and earning less than half of the income I earned before.

Nothing about what our human nature manifests is truly satisfying or fulfilling. When the jealousy, anger, and separation that our actions manifest take us to a breaking point, we find ourselves looking for a miracle, and it's important to look for those miracles in the right places. There is only one whose nature is divine, and that's God.

> For since the creation of the world God's invisible qualities—his eternal power and divine nature—have been clearly seen, being understood from what has been made, so that people are without excuse. Romans 1:20 NIV

Have you ever made excuses with God? If so, what were they?

_____

_____

_____

_____

God knows the consequences and results that we manifest from our human nature, and he doesn't want us to suffer from those consequences. Because of this desire, God extends his miracle-working ways and divine nature toward us.

> His divine power has given us everything we need for a godly life through our knowledge of him who called us by his own glory and goodness. Through these he has given us his very great and precious promises, so that through them you may participate in the divine nature, having escaped the corruption in the world caused by evil desires. 2 Peter 1:3–4 NIV

Through God's divine nature, he equips us with everything we need to live a godly life. We do not have to settle for the negativity that our human nature manifests. God invites each and every one of us to join him in participating in his divine nature. By participating in this divine nature, evil and corruption have no power over us. The evil and corruption in this world result in no good, and they don't deserve any of our attention.

The anger and jealousy I had at my new job were real, but I didn't have to allow those feelings to have any power over my life. God gave me everything I needed to live a godly life, and that godly lifestyle didn't care what job title I possessed. The world may be concerned with how much "stuff" we have, but God isn't concerned with that, and he uses us right where we are at all times.

How we utilize what we have, and whether we use what we have to bring glory to God, ranks much higher on God's list of concerns. I didn't make as much money as I did before, but I did have a much more flexible schedule and countless opportunities each day to be a light to the people who walked through the door. Gone were the days of working at a job because of anything I thought I had accomplished on my own. God had me right where he wanted me. As a result, I turned my face toward him more frequently in search of wherever it was he wanted me next.

God's desires for our lives will always be greater than the world's desires, and God can provide us with any miracle needed to fulfill those desires. God doesn't want any of us to live on our power alone. It is only by his power that we gain eternal life and as a result escape the corruption in the world caused by our evil desires.

Do you find yourself settling for anything less than what God has for you? If so, why?

_____

_____

_____

_____

What has God promised you? How do God's promises help you escape the corruption of this world?

_____

_____

_____

_____

Lesson 4: Intervention

Being human comes with a set of limitations. No matter how hard we try, we're never going to be all-knowing or all-powerful. Our time on earth is also limited for all of us. Even if we're the healthiest person alive, our days here are numbered. I'm not telling you to live an unhealthy lifestyle, because I do believe in the importance of taking care of ourselves. However, if we lived in a world that depended on humans to provide answers, some things would inevitably be left unfulfilled.

What is something in your life that remains unfulfilled, and how can you surrender that to God?

_____

_____

_____

_____

We will never be able to do it all on our own, so if we want to find fulfillment in the things that our human nature can't satisfy, we need an *intervention* from something.

Intervene: *verb* to occur incidentally so as to modify or hinder[53]

Countless sources of intervention exist in our world. No matter how big or small, we come across things that attempt to modify, hinder, or interfere with our path on just about a daily basis. While interference can be necessary in some cases, not all sources that interfere with things in our path are healthy, and we need to know how to distinguish the good from the bad.

Where are you experiencing hindrance or interference in your life, and what does it prevent you from accomplishing?

_____

_____

_____

_____

---

53 *Dictionary.com*, s.v. "Intervene," accessed December 04, 2022, https://www.dictionary.com/

You were running well. Who hindered you from obeying the truth?
Galatians 5:7 ESV

If you've ever found yourself running on the path that God has for you only to be confronted with hindrance, you're not alone. This happens all the time, because there is someone who hates it when he sees things going well, and that "someone" hindering us from obeying the truth *isn't* God.

It was not done by God, who calls you. Galatians 5:8

The enemy hates it when he sees us running well, so he tries to hinder us. His attempts of hindrance have no power over God, though! Thankfully, we have an answer to that destruction because we have a God who interferes back. Unlike Satan's interference, God's interference is divine and miraculous, and God never allows Satan to have the final say. God's interference allows us to rid ourselves of any of the enemy's attempts to hinder us from living out the life God has for us.

> *Therefore, since we are surrounded by such a great cloud of witnesses, let us throw off everything that hinders and the sin that so easily entangles. And let us run with perseverance the race marked out for us, fixing our eyes on Jesus, the pioneer and perfecter of faith. For the joy set before him he endured the cross, scorning its shame, and sat down at the right hand of the throne of God. Consider him who endured such opposition from sinners, so that you will not grow weary and lose heart. Hebrews 12:1–3 NIV*

What is something you've had to endure? Was joy present in your endurance? Why or why not?

_____

_____

_____

_____

Because of Jesus's intervention on the cross, we can throw off the entanglement of sin and not grow weary or lose heart. If that isn't miraculous, I don't know what is! The question is, are you willing to receive the miraculous intervention that Jesus offers, and in turn, willing to allow it to transform your life?

For as long as we live on this earth, Satan will not stop his attempts to hinder us, and his attempts to hinder only escalate the more that we choose to live our lives for God. Satan loved all of the shame and embarrassment I felt at my job, and he worked to make sure I felt like a failure as often as possible. He definitely succeeded in that many times, but that passage in Hebrews calls us to take on a different mindset.

Jesus knows what it's like to be tempted, face opposition, and have the enemy attempt to hinder the good works God brought him to earth to do. Unlike us, Jesus didn't allow those things to cause him to grow weary and lose heart. Rather than allow hindrance and temptation to become his master, he kept his eyes fixed on the path God laid before him, and that path included enduring the cross and opposition from sinners. Jesus endured the path God had him on and put death to shame because of the joy that was set before him. Through God's strength, we can also run the path God has us on with perseverance. The key here is that the strength comes in the race that God marks out for us, not the race we try to mark out for ourselves. God gives us the strength to run with perseverance along his path for us.

I will never claim to be a person who grew up wanting to become an author. I did not feel qualified to write a book when I felt God's call to do so, but regardless of what I felt, I was able to persevere through all of my feelings of being unqualified by fixing my eyes on what Jesus had for me in it all. Every area of my life in which I did feel qualified fell apart, while all of the areas in which I didn't feel qualified prospered. That didn't make sense from an earthly viewpoint. But it made perfect sense from God's viewpoint, because he is someone who is faithful and just to provide everything we need to run the race marked out for us.

If we fix our eyes on Jesus as we run the race marked out for us, the enemy cannot stop us from running well. Does that mean the enemy will stop trying? Of course not, which is all the more reason to keep our eyes fixed on Jesus. The enemy's attempts to hinder our lives are going to exist whether we give them attention or not, so why give him any satisfaction by letting him have any power over our lives?

Where are you experiencing weariness or losing heart right now?

_____

_____

_____

_____

What does fixing your eyes on Jesus look like for you?

_____

_____

_____

_____

Dear God,

Help me to overcome the lie of this world that says I have to do it all. You did not create me to be self-sufficient, but to rely on you and your miracle-working ways. When I am open to receiving what you have for me, there is no miracle that you can't work in my life. Thank you for sending your Son to be a first-hand display of your miraculous nature and for accomplishing the greatest miracle our world has ever seen by raising Jesus from the grave. Your nature is divine, and you invite me to participate in your divine nature so that I can escape the corruption of this world. I pray against anything attempting to hinder me from obeying your truth, because anything trying to do so is not from you. You have great and miraculous things planned for my life. I come to you now with my eyes fixed on you, the pioneer and perfecter of faith, ready to run the race you have marked for me so that I can be a vessel of your miracle-working ways to this earth.

In Jesus' name,
Amen.

Chapter Twelve

GOD IS VICTORIOUS

Lesson 1: Overcome

We live in a world that is obsessed with winning and being the best at something. Regardless of that "something," winning takes hard work and dedication. If the deadline for a goal of ours arrives and we don't come out victorious, our lack of victory can disempower us. We may begin to question whether all the time we spent working toward that goal was a waste. While I would say the answer to that question is "no," our world likes to tell us otherwise.

In order to come away victorious in any event, two or more opposing forces must be present. These forces have to want the same thing, or a battle between them doesn't exist. For two sports teams competing in a championship game, that shared desire looks like a trophy and a championship title. For a group of people competing in a political race, they share a desire to win office.

Battles occur everywhere we look in our physical world. While battles in our physical world affect each of us on a daily basis, those aren't the only battles affecting us. Battles exist in the spiritual realm too. We all fight battles in our lives regularly, and God also fights battles for us. What exactly does God battle for, and who does he battle against?

If we asked a Christian what they loved about God, it wouldn't take long for us to hear some version of the fact that he loves us enough to die for us. I agree that it is amazing that Jesus died for us, but what makes it amazing? Thinking about Jesus dying for us in the context of fighting battles, when Jesus died and rose from the grave on the third day, he declared *victory* over death. That alone is incredible news, but what does Jesus gaining victory over death say about God's character? How does someone obtain victory?

Victory: *noun* the overcoming of an enemy or an antagonist; achievement of mastery or success in a struggle or endeavor[54]

The first way to achieve victory we will address is by *overcoming*.

Recall a time you were victorious; what did you overcome to obtain that victory?

_____

_____

_____

_____

What makes God's victorious nature so great? To understand its greatness, we must first understand God's enemy and what God overcame.

> *When Jesus had left the crowd and gone indoors, his disciples came to him and said, "Tell us what the parable about the weeds in the field means." Jesus answered, "The man who sowed the good seed is the Son of Man; the field is the world; the good seed is the people who belong to the Kingdom; the weeds are the people who belong to the Evil One; and the enemy who sowed the weeds is the Devil. The harvest is the end of the age, and the harvest workers are angels. Matthew 13:36–39*

God and Satan are enemies of each other. They're both fighting a battle, and they are both fighting over *us*! Both the good seed that belonged to God and the weeds that belonged to Satan represented people. God and Satan both want as big of a harvest as possible. The question is, who gets the victory?

Whoever gets victory depends on who we allow to have victory. The goodness of God and the evil of Satan are both more powerful than us. While

---

54   *Merriam-Webster's Dictionary and Thesaurus,* Updated Edition, s.v. "Victory."

they are both more powerful than us, only one of them is more powerful than the other.

Do not be overcome by evil, but overcome evil with good. Romans 12:21 NIV

How have you seen good overcome evil in your own life?

_____

_____

_____

_____

This passage shows us two possible victories. Either we let evil have its victory over us and be like the weeds, or we have victory over evil with good and be like the good seed. On our own strength, overcoming evil with good isn't possible. God knows we can't overcome evil on our own, and that's when he steps in to help us.

If we want to live life victoriously on this earth, we have to invite the power that has victory over every other power into our lives, and that's God. We have to shift our mindset on what it looks like to truly live victoriously. Living victoriously in God's eyes does not look like winning over the approval of the world, because we will never achieve that victory. The world did not always approve of Jesus's lifestyle, and it won't always approve of ours if we live as God calls us to, so it's best if we stop waiting for the world to change its mind and act as God calls us to anyway.

My relationship with God forever changed when I realized that God *wants* me to have victory, and whenever I do what he asks of me, I *can't* lose. When God asked me to give up certain areas of my life to pursue a different lifestyle career, he didn't see me giving up those things as a "loss" but as a *gain*. What did I gain? I gained space in my mind to hear God's thoughts, because I spent a lot less energy trying to make something out of nothing in my career. I also gained the space emotionally to be more available for people—especially in being an advocate for sexual assault survivors—because I was less concerned with holding up a certain image and being involved in places like my former career that did nothing but drain me emotionally.

Battling and claiming victory over the evil in this world is not a one-time event, but a lifestyle. Satan and his attempts to bring us down will not disappear from this earth anytime soon. We need to keep our faith in the one who overcame evil in order to continue to have victory over evil in our lives.

In fact, this is love for God: to keep his commands. And his commands are not burdensome, for everyone born of God overcomes the world. This is the victory that has overcome the world, even our faith. Who is it that overcomes the world? Only the one who believes that Jesus is the Son of God. 1 John 5:3–5 NIV

Only one person to ever walk this earth had victory over death, and that's Jesus. God shares that victory over death with us so that we gain the power to overcome this world too. How do we earn that victory over death? Faith. Jesus already *won* the battle over the enemy! All we have to do is have faith and believe in Jesus as the Son of God. In doing so, we share in his victory and have the power to overcome this world.

If Satan knows that good overcomes evil, and that he's already lost to God, why do you think he keeps trying?

_____

_____

_____

_____

Why do you think God shares his victory to overcome the world with us? What does that say about his character?

_____

_____

_____

_____

How has your faith in Jesus helped you overcome a battle you've faced in life?

_____

_____

_____

_____

Lesson 2: Mastery

At the completion of graduate school, a few of my classmates put together a slideshow with everyone from our cohort. The slideshow included an individual picture of each of us along with a nickname at the bottom. On that day, I received the nickname "the human calculator." How did I earn that nickname? Not from anything I did in graduate school, but from what I did as a child.

I *mastered* my times tables at a young age by spending many hours practicing with flash cards and playing math-based computer games. My mastery of mental math led me to many victories over the years. I emerged victorious so many times while playing math-based games in class that my elementary school teachers sometimes intentionally asked me to sit out just to give another classmate the opportunity to emerge victorious.

What do you consider yourself a master of, and how have you seen victory from it?

_____

_____

_____

_____

> **Mastery:** *noun* the authority of a master; dominion[55]

---

55 *Merriam-Webster's Dictionary and Thesaurus,* Updated Edition, s.v. "Mastery."

Achieving mastery includes the elements of authority and dominion. In order for God to be victorious in nature, he must also have the authority of a master. In both the Old Testament and the New Testament, the Bible speaks of the nature of God's authority; the following comes from the book of Daniel:

> *During this vision in the night, I saw what looked like a human being. He was approaching me, surrounded by clouds, and he went to the one who had been living forever and was presented to him. He was given authority, honor, and royal power, so that the people of all nations, races, and languages would serve him. His authority would last forever, and his kingdom would never end. Daniel 7:13–14*

Daniel's vision prophesies of a human who is given authority and served by people of all nations. John had a similar vision that is recorded in Revelation:

> *After this I looked, and there was an enormous crowd—no one could count all the people! They were from every race, tribe, nation, and language, and they stood in front of the throne and of the Lamb, dressed in white robes and holding palm branches in their hands. They called out in a loud voice: "Salvation comes from our God, who sits on the throne, and from the Lamb!" Revelation 7:9–10*

Daniel mentions in his vision a human who has authority in a kingdom that never ends. John brings light to this same person that people of all nations will serve, and he calls that person the Lamb. The person both Daniel and John have visions of is Jesus, the Lamb of God.

We know God has a kingdom, and we know Jesus has authority in this kingdom. The question is, why would we want to join God in his kingdom to begin with? What benefit comes from serving God? To answer these questions, we must better understand God's victorious nature and mastery.

> *For he has rescued us from the dominion of darkness and brought us into the kingdom of the Son he loves, in whom we have redemption, the forgiveness of sins. Colossians 1:13–14 NIV*

Regardless of whatever or whoever we allow to be our "master," we all have a master. None of us is powerful enough to control everything in our lives, and we never will be. In other words, we will always be subject to the authority of something outside of ourselves. What authority should we allow to be our master?

These verses paint for us a picture of two different masters—sin and God. Sin comes from our human nature, and all of us at some point have subjected ourselves to the authority and dominion of its darkness. God isn't satisfied with sin being the only option we can choose as our master. Instead, God gives us another option. He sacrificed his Son's life for ours and offers us salvation to join him in his kingdom.

What prevents you from letting God have full authority in your life?

_____

_____

_____

_____

This redemption and the forgiveness of our sins sounds great, but what gives Jesus the authority to offer us that redemption?

> *For we know that our old self was crucified with him so that the body ruled by sin might be done away with, that we should no longer be slaves to sin—because anyone who has died has been set free from sin. Now if we died with Christ, we believe that we will also live with him. For we know that since Christ was raised from the dead, he cannot die again; death no longer has mastery over him. The death he died, he died to sin once for all; but the life he lives, he lives to God.*
> *Romans 6:6–10 NIV*

Jesus died for all of our sins, rose, and achieved mastery over death. By gaining this mastery, Jesus reigns victorious over death, and nothing can ever take that victory away from him! Jesus shares his victory over death with us. If we die with Christ—or receive his death as a payment for our sin—we also get to live with him in his kingdom. God's kingdom consists of never-ending life, and he loves every one of us enough to rescue us from the dominion of darkness to share that eternal life with us.

To share in that eternal life with Jesus, we must invite him to be the master of our lives, so we can quit allowing sin and death to have mastery over us. How do we do that? We have to quit thinking our way of life and human nature has something better in store for us than what God has in store for our lives. If doing things "our way" was truly the best thing for us, then our world would be significantly less broken than it is today, because our world makes many more decisions from doing things "our way" rather than God's way.

Allowing Jesus to be the master of my life looked like pursuing a life full of things that I didn't see myself as a "master" in. While one might think that living a life full of things you don't think you're a master in would result in defeat, when Jesus is involved, it's not defeating, it's *freeing*. I finally reached a place where I realized that at the end of the day, the only one I was accountable to for my life was God. If God, my master, was pleased with what I did, then nothing else mattered. Do I consider myself an expert in this? Certainly not, but the freedom gained from this mindset makes every trial experienced on this earth worth it.

What do you think it means to "die with Christ?"

_____

_____

_____

_____

Have you been set free from the mastery of sin? What was the result of that victory?

_____

_____

_____

_____

Lesson 3: Success

Our world has an extremely unhealthy desire for seeking and finding victory. Why do I say that? I say that because another angle of victory comes from achieving *success*. In the messages our world portrays, success looks like getting the education, finding a life partner, making it in the corporate world, buying a house, and starting a family. Easy enough, right?

As someone who so far has really achieved only one of the items on that list, I'm going to have to say that it's not. Do I think my life isn't a success because of it? No, I don't. However, there are plenty of people in this world who do feel like a failure because they haven't lived up to the world's standards for victory and success, and it's time to start breaking down those standards!

Success: *noun* favorable or desired outcome[56]

When have you previously achieved a desired outcome in your life, and how did you feel victorious as a result?

_____

_____

_____

_____

What is a desired outcome you have for your life now?

_____

_____

_____

_____

The world we live in sets high standards for success that many of us will never feel victorious from, but God's desired outcome looks a little different from the world's. To get an idea of God's "favorable and desired outcome," let's look at the story of Adam and Eve.

---

56 *Merriam-Webster's Dictionary and Thesaurus,* Updated Edition, s.v. "Success."

The LORD God took the man and put him in the Garden of Eden to work it and take care of it. And the LORD God commanded the man, "You are free to eat from any tree in the garden; but you must not eat from the tree of the knowledge of good and evil, for when you eat from it you will certainly die." Genesis 2:15–17 NIV

This interaction between God and Adam comes before sin entered the world. Our separation from God has yet to occur, and in God's words to Adam, God shares his desired outcomes for the world. God tells Adam that he is *free* to eat from any tree in the garden except for the tree of the knowledge of good and evil—God desires *freedom*.

The only thing Adam had to do in order to maintain his freedom was to not eat fruit from one specific tree. God telling Adam *not* to do something may not come off as "freeing," but why did God say that?

To answer that question, we look to one of God's other desires—the desire for *life*. God warned Adam that he would die if he ate from the tree of the knowledge of good and evil. God doesn't want us to die, he wants us to *live* and to live *freely*.

Why do you think God's desires are for us to have life and to be free?

_____

_____

_____

_____

We could walk up to any random person and ask if they desire both life and freedom, and I can guarantee that person would say yes. Freedom and life are both desires that we all share with God, so why don't we see more of them in our world? There isn't more life and freedom in our world because we try to obtain these desires our own way rather than by God's way. We don't like being told not to do something, and Adam and Eve were no different. They didn't listen to God's caution—they ate from that one specific tree. When they ate the fruit from the tree of the knowledge of good and evil, sin entered the world, and they lost both their life and freedom.

And the LORD God said, "The man has now become like one of us, knowing good and evil. He must not be allowed to reach out his

hand and take also from the tree of life and eat, and live forever."
Genesis 3:22 NIV

If the Bible ended there, God wouldn't look victorious or like much of a success, would he? Adam and Eve went against God's will, and instead of freedom and life, they earned death—the same death we all earn from our sin.

To our benefit, God doesn't let Adam and Eve have the final say—he is a God of restoration. God wants us to be with him, to be free, and to live eternally. Despite us breaking God's commands, God successfully restores our possibility to share his desires.

"Very truly I tell you, whoever hears my word and believes him who
sent me has eternal life and will not be judged but has crossed over
from death to life." John 5:24 NIV

None of us asked for our lives or brought ourselves to life, so to think we have the answers that lead to life is nothing short of ignorance and selfishness. We can no longer achieve eternal life by eating from the tree of life, but we can achieve it through Jesus! Jesus defeated death, and he invites each of us to do the same by believing in him. To find success, or the favorable and desired outcome for our lives, we must turn our eyes to God, because he alone offers that favor and success.

Let the favor of the Lord our God be upon us, and establish the work of
our hands upon us; yes, establish the work of our hands! Psalm 90:17 ESV

Success came in my life once I started allowing God to establish the work of my hands. I don't claim to be a wordsmith (even though no one I meet ever believes me when I say that, because I'm an author), and I don't pretend to be a person who thinks I am good with words when sitting down to write my books. Instead, whenever I write, I ask God to give me *his* words. God faithfully provides those words, and as a result, I have seen success in my writing. By the grace of God, both *Broken Lenses: Identifying Your Truth in a World of Lies* and *Broken Lenses, Volume 2: Seeing Others' Value in a World of Division* have won awards and are available in bookstores nation-wide.

Our world will never agree with God on what success looks like, so we all have to actively make the choice about which version of "success" we will pursue. The world cannot promise us that we will achieve the favorable outcome it desires, but God can make that promise, so if you ask me, I'm following God's road to success. It's not a coincidence that I have found success doing something that the world told me over and over again that I would fail at—because God *doesn't* lose.

Have you ever been in a situation where you struggled to see God leading you to a favorable outcome? If so, what was it?

_____

_____

_____

_____

Have you seen God bring restoration in your own life? If so, how?

_____

_____

_____

_____

～

Lesson 4: Struggle

Have you ever been in a situation and wondered when it would ever end? Me too. The world we live in doesn't always deal us a desirable hand. We've all been there, and we all know what I'm talking about when I say, "The *struggle* is real." What does "the struggle" look like? Well, it's different for each of us, but no matter the cause, nobody enjoys struggling.

Whether we enjoy them or not, the struggles in this world aren't going away until Jesus comes back and heaven and earth are restored. Even though we cannot completely eradicate struggle in this world, we *can* change our mindset toward struggles.

What is a struggle from which you have found victory? How did you obtain that victory?

_____

_____

_____

_____

How could you use victory from something with which you are currently struggling?

_____

_____

_____

Instead of taking on our traditional view of what a "struggle" is, I want to challenge everyone to take on God's mindset.

Finally, be strong in the Lord and in his mighty power. Put on the full armor of God, so that you can take your stand against the devil's schemes. For our struggle is not against flesh and blood, but against the rulers, against the authorities, against the powers of this dark world and against the spiritual forces of evil in the heavenly realms. Ephesians 6:10–12 NIV

Those verses acknowledge the fact that our world has struggles. The struggles mentioned aren't related to things "being difficult" or "not going our way." This passage shows us that other human beings are _not_ the source of our struggle—Satan is.

Why do you think Paul makes sure to include that our struggle is not against other humans?

_____

_____

_____

_____

The enemy's schemes led Adam and Eve to eat the forbidden fruit, and he's up to those same schemes with us today. Satan *loves* to see us struggle, and he's not going to stop his schemes any time soon!

I knew very early on in my author journey while writing my first book that *Broken Lenses* was not going to just be one book, but rather three books. I encountered many struggles over the six years that it took me to write this series, but those struggles didn't come from the people around me. The struggles I faced while writing came from an enemy who really hates that I'm exposing his evil ways in all three of those books! Thankfully, by the power of God, we have the ability to stand victorious over Satan's schemes.

> *Therefore put on the full armor of God, so that when the day of evil comes, you may be able to stand your ground, and after you have done everything, to stand. Stand firm then, with the belt of truth buckled around your waist, with the breastplate of righteousness in place, and with your feet fitted with the readiness that comes from the gospel of peace. In addition to all this, take up the shield of faith, with which you can extinguish all the flaming arrows of the evil one. Take the helmet of salvation and the sword of the Spirit, which is the word of God. Ephesians 6:13–17 NIV*

As much as Satan loves to see us struggle, God loves to see us stand victorious. Putting on God's armor to protect us is the *only* armor qualified to protect us as we fight against Satan's schemes. God *wants* us to be victorious, and he makes his armor available to everyone, but it's up to us to put on that armor. There is no spiritual attack that Satan sends our way that God's shield of faith can't extinguish. We have no need to reinvent God's armor. The battle has already been *won*; we just need to keep our mind fixed on God!

My desire for ministry started because God brought me out of my deepest struggle and redefined the way I saw myself. Satan loved the way that I saw myself after being raped all those years ago—as undesirable, ugly, unlovable, and forever tainted. The struggle to see myself any other way lasted for years. After finding my faith in God again, I used that shield of faith to extinguish the flaming arrows of lies that Satan shot my way to cause me to believe those things of myself. God has not only healed me from my own struggles of being a sexual assault survivor, but he also now allows me to help other survivors.

All three of the *Broken Lenses* books now exist because my struggles stood no chance against God's mercy, kindness, and light. Satan and his lies are not more powerful than God's truth and sovereignty, and they never will be! I know God has called me to minister to survivors, and I welcome all opportunities I get to share my own story of being a rape survivor. Why? Not because I want people to feel sorry for me, but because sharing my story of healing and the victory that God has given me allows other people to have hope that they can find that same victory over the darkness in their life.

God doesn't want just me to experience the freedom that comes from his victory, he wants *you* to experience that freedom, too! You were brought to this world for a reason, and nothing you do will change the love God has for you or the way he sees you. My prayer for all of you is that you find the benefit in getting to know God and in putting on his armor. Evil exists in our world everywhere we look, and the only way we stand a chance in defeating that evil is through God's goodness and mercy. God always has your best interest in mind. You are God's masterpiece, and I pray against anything in this world that tries to tell you otherwise!

Of the pieces of God's armor—the belt of truth, breastplate of righteousness, readiness of the gospel of peace, shield of faith, helmet of salvation, and sword of the Spirit—which could you use more of in your life, and why?

_____

_____

_____

_____

Which of the pieces of God's armor have you used in a past struggle, and how did you see victory as a result?

_____

_____

_____

_____

Dear God,

You are an overcomer, and you defeated both death and evil when you raised Jesus from the grave. My sinful nature is evil, and without your goodness, my sin overtakes me. Thank you for offering me your goodness and the opportunity to have victory over my sin. All authority in heaven and on earth belongs to Jesus, and anything or anyone attempting to be victorious without your involvement will ultimately fail. Thank you for your willingness to rescue me from the dominion of darkness through redemption and the forgiveness of my sins. There is an enemy of this world who wants to see me fail and struggle, but your armor allows me to stand victorious against his schemes. Putting on your armor is the only way I can be victorious over Satan, so I ask that you show me how I can better equip myself with your armor. There is no battle I have gone through that was too difficult for you to win, and there never will be a battle that is too difficult for you.

In Jesus' name,
Amen.

CALL TO ACTION

For more from Emily, check out the first two books of the *Broken Lenses* series, follow her on Instagram @emilybernathauthor, and visit www.emilybernathauthor.com

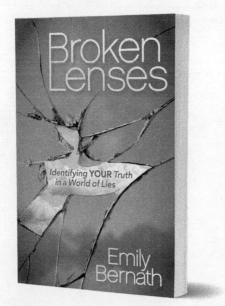

About the Author

A devoted advocate for survivors of sexual assault—and a rape survivor herself—Emily Bernath began writing out of her passion for women's ministry. Her personal tragedy led her into periods of darkness that she was only able to move beyond with the support of others and the healing power of Jesus. After rediscovering her faith and identity in Christ, Emily was able to discover freedom from the shame, condemnation, and abuse she experienced. Today, she lives to be a resource for other sexual assault survivors and help them find that same freedom.

Emily has spoken at many events, radio shows, and been featured on FOX 13 Salt Lake City in her advocacy work. She teaches classes to other advocates about the spiritual impact of sexual assault and how faith plays a role in a survivor's healing journey. Emily is currently pursuing a master's degree in social work from Utah Valley University. She also supports survivors by serving on the board of Reveal to Heal International—a faith-based non-profit that seeks to address sexual abuse prevention and awareness.

Before beginning her career as an author, she earned a bachelor's degree in chemistry and a master's degree in business administration. When she's not writing, Emily enjoys drinking good coffee, playing soccer and softball, sup-

porting her local church, and connecting with other people to hear their sto-
ries. While she is originally from the Toledo, OH area, she currently resides in
Salt Lake City, UT.

A free ebook edition is available with the purchase of this book.

To claim your free ebook edition:

1. Visit MorganJamesBOGO.com
2. Sign your name CLEARLY in the space
3. Complete the form and submit a photo of the entire copyright page
4. You or your friend can download the ebook to your preferred device

A **FREE** ebook edition is available for you or a friend with the purchase of this print book.

_____

CLEARLY SIGN YOUR NAME ABOVE

Instructions to claim your free ebook edition:
1. Visit MorganJamesBOGO.com
2. Sign your name CLEARLY in the space above
3. Complete the form and submit a photo of this entire page
4. You or your friend can download the ebook to your preferred device

Print & Digital Together Forever.

Snap a photo   Free ebook   Read anywhere